AF255734

THE COURTS WE BUILT

The Battle for a Tennis Cathedral

Douglas McCarty

2026

Contents

Foreword
by Tom Greider

You probably think there's a huge difference between an indoor tennis facility and a cathedral. So did I, until I read one of Doug's chapters—Why (Y) Tennis? The Cathedral and the Museum.

I arrived at the Eugene Family YMCA Tennis Center in April of 1983, about three years after a group of tennis lovers financed it, built it, and handed it to the YMCA to steward that gift for the people of Eugene.

Four indoor courts, a community of players, and a soul that grew stronger every year. By the time I left, we had over 250 members, more than 100 juniors in our programs, and an adult conditioning class that—forty-three years later—still meets on Tuesday and Thursday lunchtimes. I still play in it.

What Doug McCarty has written here is not just the history of that building. It is the story of what happens when a community builds something with its own hands and its own money, watches it become irreplaceable, and then has to fight to keep it from being repurposed by the very institution entrusted to protect it. He also writes about the deeper meaning of the ancient and yet still modern game of tennis, and about dreams old tennis players still have for kids who have not yet been born.

Doug is a problem solver, not a complainer, although some of his complaints are epic. This book doesn't just diagnose what's wrong. It offers a way forward—a win-win that will honor the donors, the members, and the YMCA itself. Whether the current board has the wisdom to accept it remains to be seen.

Read it. Then decide whose side you're on.

Acknowledgments

This book is for the tennis community of Eugene —
past, present, and future.

For those who dreamed the courts into being in 1977,
opened their checkbooks without being asked, and built
something that did not yet exist. Some of them are gone
now. They deserve better stewardship of the tennis
cathedral than they are receiving these days.

For those who have played there across five decades
— the juniors who learned the game on those four courts,
the adults who found their footing, the Tuesday and
Thursday regulars who have shown up for forty-three
years and are still showing up. You are the living proof
that the building matters.

For those who are fighting to keep it now — who
have written letters, attended meetings, asked hard
questions, and refused to accept that a community asset
built with private money can simply be repurposed by an
institution that did not build it and does not fully
understand what it holds.

And for the young players who have not yet arrived —
the eighteen-year-old who will drive into Eugene in 2042
and look for a court, the kids born in 2035 who will
discover in tennis a passion that will propel them to great
heights, and the coaches who will see something in
students each year that the students cannot yet see in
themselves.

The courts are still there. This book is an argument
for keeping them.

Prologue: The Broken Dog

I was heading home from college in November, 1973. To almost all of us of age at the time it was a golden era: no home computers, no cell phones or internet, Vietnam was ratcheting down, coming to an end, the Eagles were singing *Take It Easy* and Elton was singing *Benny and the Jets* and I was northbound on US 29 in Virginia. That's when I saw him, shivering and odd shaped just inside the slow lane. A dog, alive but maybe not for long, mangled by a car that was long gone. Perhaps the driver didn't even hear the impact; maybe he was blasting *Benny and the Jets.*

I stopped on the shoulder and jogged back. Farther ahead a truck had stopped and I expected to see the trucker soon, but if we left the dog there just a few moments more another car would finish him. I knelt and wrapped the dog in my army jacket—we all wore army surplus jackets back then—and gently got him off the road. At the very end, he couldn't take it any more, stretched out and bit me, and I swore softly, recalling what the road to hell was paved with. Now the trucker was kneeling beside me and said he would take the dog to a vet nearby, a place he knew. I was still three or four hours from Philadelphia. I watched as he placed the dog in his cab, got in and drove away.

At that moment I shivered and realized my jacket was riding away with the trucker and the dog. So, in the end, I lost my jacket, a dog bit me, and the dog most likely died or was put to sleep anyway. Oh for three, as they say.

This little book of mine about our local tennis cathedral is not a story about futility, and it is not a story about ingratitude. If the dog had not been in so much pain I think he would have wagged his tail and thanked me with his eyes, the way dogs do. That's the difference between dogs and people; dogs at least have a fundamental urge to say thank you. No, I think this will be is a story about what you do when something worth saving is in the road. Just as with the dog in the road, I'm not sure yet how it ends; I only know the little role I am supposed to play. Ergo, this book.

This book will tell you a tale about a town in 1977 that I had never heard of—at the time I was living deep in the Korean mountains as a Peace Corps Volunteer, having the time of my life. It was literally a village, a "li" 里 (리). But the American town, now my town, Eugene, Oregon was just about to receive the nicest gift any rainy town could: a fully paid-for, indoor tennis facility, for the YMCA to run. Apparently 36 guys got together in what were pretty squirrelly economic times, opened up their checkbooks and made it happen.

The Tennis Center is a magic place that, to be honest, doesn't look all that magic. Maybe that's the best kind of magic place, something incognito, in camouflage, cruising under the radar.

I landed in Eugene in 1995 and when the rains came, suddenly appreciated the chance to play tennis high and dry from the weather, the rain and the snow. And for thirty-one years I have done exactly that. And now, at my age I was hoping to play another ten years and then be one of those fogies who "used to play, but doesn't anymore."

I think the best way to tell the current drama and situation is to just write these things up, chapter by chapter, in my own style, occasionally drawing from great minds—Orwell, Whitman, Blake—to illustrate a point or just to add some gravitas—Lord knows I've never had an oversupply of my own gravitas. By the end of this book you will know everything I know. And the situation will have yet to resolve itself. The YMCA has placed itself at odds with its ethical, legal and reputational obligations, and in opposition to our little tennis community. And me.

It's so odd, because I am the best ally the Eugene YMCA could ever find. But for now, I've stopped the car, I've taken off my jacket and tried to wrap them up before they make a grave mistake—ethical mistakes are always the worst. I may still get bit and lose my jacket. The tennis community may do everything right and we still lose our beloved center. The fifteen thousand people who don't know yet that they need this place—some forty-year-old with a family who walks in out of the rain in 2037—may never get the chance.

People in the tennis community have confided how depressing it all is, how hopeless it seems. Personally, I like our odds in this fight. There is something about being on the ethical, legal and correct reputational side, while facing the big bureaucracy with its slogans and paid consultants that makes me think it will be a good fight for us and a not so good one for them.

Chapter 1: The Courts We Built

The Genesis of a Tennis Center

————

A note before we begin: what follows are the actual imagined conversations lifted from almost fifty years ago. Names have not been changed.

————

Eugene, Oregon. November, 1978. Two guys, Stan and Nate, watching the rain fall.

————

Nate, you know what bugs me?

What.

Rain. This dang rain, every single year I've lived in this town. You can dam the damn rivers but you can't dam the damn clouds.

Stan, you know, everybody complains about the weather but nobody ever—

Yeah, yeah, I know. But I got an idea.

Oh boy. Here we go.

I keep getting this dream. Seriously, it's a real dream. and when I wake up I remember it. Anyway, you know how the tennis club across town has those covered courts? And the Ducks have their own covered courts, right next to Mac Court?

Yeah?

We oughtta build us some. Covered courts. For everybody. In my dream we're all playing in the courts, all lit up, and when we finish we head out into the November rain, dark, cold, unpleasant. So, a building with tennis courts inside.

That's the dream?

Yup.

That sounds expensive, and who would run it?

That's the funny part. It's just a barn, Nate. Just a barn. That's all we need.

I thought you said it would be tennis courts, like a tennis—

—center. A tennis center.

Tennis center, but really just a barn?

Well, that's all it is. My brother-in-law down in Roseburg put one up — calls it a butler building, or something like that. From green field to finished in about three months. He's got his storage in there, even his office.

The farmer guy? What did it cost him?

Rancher, actually. And not much, really. He told me he made all his money on it back in a year, from all the sales he could make out of that protected space. No more wet grain, spoiled valley grass, rodent visits.

Huh.

It locks up tighter than a convent, Nate. I'm telling you.

————

Six months later. Second floor, the YMCA offices on Patterson Street. Stan and the Director, Bill.

————

So let me get this straight, Stan. You—your group—want to build us a tennis center on that swampy piece of land that runs from 21st to 22nd?

Yup. We've got about twenty, thirty guys ready to pay in, we've got the plans drawn up, and Nate knows the folks in planning — that won't be a problem. It's a dirt simple plan.

And the Y members can join the tennis thing, too, right?

Yup, just pay their fees.

And the Y doesn't have to pay? Cause, you know. You know what interest rates are right now?

Yah, some of them are hitting sixteen percent, and the banks are pulling their loans. I heard a lot of ranches and farms are in serious trouble — in fact, every single one of them that borrowed from the banksters to finance herds, buy big iron. It's not going to be pretty.

Stan, in these times we don't have the money.

Bill. I already told you. Twice. The Y won't have to pay. Not one red cent. Turnkey.

I suppose you'll need an office or something. Bathrooms. Electricity. And the courts themselves—

Bill. You're the YMCA. You've been running things in this town since 1950. We build it — office and bathrooms included — you run it. And, by the way, tennis pretty much runs itself, once you get a reservation book going. Like a Swiss watch. Tennis players don't need any hand holding, no coaching. No lifeguards, nobody on site to stop kids fighting on a basketball court.

Okay, yeah, I get it.

And tennis players, well, you know their credit is good going forward to support this place, membership and all that.

Okay.

So. Do we have a deal?

————

Fall, 1979. Some weeks before the doors open. Nate and Stan are at lunch.

————

Hey, Stan. I been thinking.

Uh oh.

No, look. We raised this money, built this thing, the Y says they're gonna run it as a tennis center for all of Eugene — not just the swells at the tennis club. Anybody can walk in off the street, join the Y, pay the extra fee. No tennis whites required, no waiting list, no membership bonds or membership jackets.

That's the whole idea, Nate. That's always been the whole idea.

I know. But here's what I keep turning over. What if — just what if — the Y pulls a fast one on us? Say, after five years they decide they need it for something else, or they figure they can make more money renting it out. What if they just decide they don't care about tennis anymore?

That's ridiculous, Nate. It's a tennis center. That's all it can be used for. We have a deal.

Stan, you said it yourself — we built them a barn with some nets and some courts in it. Four walls, a roof. What if they change their minds someday, decide to "go in a different direction"?

What direction?

I dunno. Racquetball. Handball. That crazy jazzercise thing. Things change, Stan.

Look, if you can't trust the YMCA, who can you trust? Seriously. It's like a church. It's got the word Christian right in the name. Is something calling itself Christian going to swindle you out of a tennis center we gave them? For free?

Yeah, sure. But I know what it's like in my business, so—

This is the Y, for crying out loud, not like the people you have to deal with.

Okay. Maybe. But should we at least get something in writing? A contract, an operating agreement, a memorandum of some kind?

Nope, we have a solid deal, handshake with the YMCA. End of discussion, to me. I am not going to spend my life getting fussy with bureaucrats and their paperwork. We — you and I — did this to play tennis. And to give this town a place to play tennis.

Stan—

Who knows, Nate? Maybe the next Arthur Ashe is already born right here in Eugene, has his first little kid racquet in his hand right now. Maybe the next Chrissie Evert is out there somewhere, some third grader in the rain who just needs a dry court and somebody to show

her the game. And whoever the next Jimmy Connors is —
it might as well be a kid who learned how right here on
these courts.

You don't even like Connors.

Nobody has to like Connors. The point is, twenty
years from now, or thirty, the best players on earth could
be getting their start on courts we built. Just imagine
that.

I'd rather just imagine beating you at doubles.

Ha. Well. Keep dreaming. The point is — Nate, if you
can't trust the Y to do the basic Christian thing, to do
what it promised, then we've got problems way bigger
than some butler building we handed them on a silver
platter.

A pause.

Okay. You're probably right.

I know I'm right.

————

And so they built it. A butler barn, only for tennis.
Four covered courts, dry as a bone in the Eugene rain,
open to anyone with clean shoes and a racquet. The Y ran
it, and the tennis community was as good as its word. For
decades, the Tennis Center was the place where kids
learned to play. Old men kept their knees going a few
extra years. Ladies with kids in school discovered the
game and a passion for it. Leagues formed and dissolved
and reformed. Generations of Eugeneans who would
never in their lives have set foot at the tennis club found
out they loved this game. In 2022 there were roughly 500
tennis center members, whose fees contributed about
$450,000 per year to the top line.

All based on a handshake and almost 50 years of
good faith, and 36 special people who had a vision and
acted on it.

A handshake.

The pen, as it turned out, would have been the wiser instrument.

But that part of the story comes later.

————

Postscript

A rough accounting.

The facility opened in 1980 and operated as a public tennis center through approximately 2022 — a span of roughly forty-two years. Based on conservative estimates of membership across those decades:

In the early years (1980–1995), a growing community facility likely served between 150 and 250 members annually. Over fifteen years, that's roughly 2,250 to 3,750 member-years of tennis.

In its peak middle years (1995–2010), with Eugene's population growing and recreational tennis near its national apex, a realistic estimate of 350 to 500 members per year yields another 5,250 to 7,500 member-years across fifteen years.

In its later years (2010–2022), a stable and loyal core of 400 to 500 members per year — confirmed by the 2022 figure of roughly 500 members — represents another 4,800 to 6,000 member-years.

Total estimated member-years served across four decades: somewhere between 12,000 and 17,000. That counts members only. It does not count walk-ins, USTA league players, competition nights, junior programs, or the children of members who grew up on those courts. The real number of lives touched is considerably higher.

That is what was built. That is the gift that the tennis community both gave and received, and the gift that requires the community's stewardship today.

That is what the Y began to dismantle in 2022.

The two men who stood in the rain and dreamed of a dry court for everybody — their names, along with thirty-four others, were written on a plaque, to honor and remember them. In 2022 the Y renamed the Tennis Center to include "pickleball," placed the plaque in a dank hallway near the bathroom for a while, next to the cleaning closet. And then quietly either put it away or threw it away.

All we have for certain now is a photograph.

Chapter 2: The Cadge Creep Society

"You can act like a man." — The Godfather (Don Vito Corleone to Johnny Fontane)

Yesterday, some organization calling themselves The Eugene Parks Foundation sent me an email.

It was cheerful, glossy, and upbeat—full of photographs of sunlit paths and happy people. It read just like a university alumni magazine—we currently get four of those—except digitized and more aggressively friendly. There were updates on programs—conservation efforts, new plantings—and, of course, multiple buttons inviting me to donate. You could even give crypto or stock shares, if that's what you had lying around with no better use in mind. Crypto, indeed.

People already pay high property taxes. City management is uneven at best. The parks themselves are dirtier and less safe than they should be. There are straightforward, professional solutions—contracted landscaping, cleaning, maintenance—which would no doubt save taxpayers' money. Private companies do this every day, efficiently and without emotional theater.

But that wasn't what the email was offering. It wasn't asking for a solution. It was asking for my emotional commitment to those beautiful pictures. It asked me to "be part of the mission." I was free to give almost anything, it seemed. And for some sort of status, I could pledge $1,200 a year for three years and become a member of the "Legacy Circle." I could even remember the parks in my estate planning.

This is not a request. It is an appeal.

It is the latest version of what I've come to think of as cadge creep: the normalization of begging—politely, cheerfully, with implied moral authority—for money that people already worked for and paid taxes on.

"Fundraising" used to mean something specific. It meant raising money for a shared necessity that couldn't reasonably be financed through ordinary exchange: bonds for a school or a firehouse, a hospital wing, disaster relief. It implied urgency, limitation, and accountability.

Today, the word has been laundered. It now covers everything from municipal shortfalls to personal ambition. Asking has replaced producing. Cadging for dollars is now a career. Moral framing has replaced value exchange. If the cause is described warmly enough, the question of whether the money should be asked for at all disappears.

————

Some years ago, a teenage boy rang my doorbell.

He wasn't selling anything, not really. He announced —almost rehearsed—that he was going to the London School of Economics for a year abroad. He offered no proof that he was going; all he held was a clipboard and a couple of well-wrinkled pieces of paper.

He explained that London was expensive and he was fundraising. He had magazines I could subscribe to, or I could simply give him twenty dollars.

The pitch was intimate and presumptive, as though the moral groundwork had already been laid.

I asked where he lived. He hesitated. Then gestured vaguely over his shoulder—a couple of blocks away. I asked what street. He grew uncomfortable and tried to redirect the conversation.

Was I going to buy a magazine, or give him the money?

I declined.

What stayed with me wasn't the kid—though I have doubts he ever went to London, or even intended to. What stayed with me was my next-door neighbor's response when I mentioned the encounter. She smiled and said she'd met him, too. He seemed like such a nice boy. She gave him forty dollars, cash. She hoped he'd have a wonderful trip.

That moment crystallized something I'd been noticing for decades: the quiet normalization of begging. And the corresponding erosion of the idea that money is something you earn by working for it: finding a job, doing the work.

Slowly. Almost invisibly.

————

When I was young, I earned money in ordinary ways. I walked a neighbor's dog. I sold seeds and greeting cards door to door. I delivered the local paper before dawn. I worked the night shift at KFC. All of this before I turned sixteen. This was not an act of virtue on my part—it was simply the only way a kid, age 7 to 15, could get any money.

It never occurred to me to walk through neighborhoods and ask strangers to pony up for something I wanted.

If it became known to my friends, I would have been ashamed. My parents would have been furious—asking publicly would have implied that our family couldn't pay its way, that we depended on the charity of others. In our own neighborhood.

That line mattered once.

Work implied reciprocity. Effort implied dignity. Work was hard, and that was built into the system, and that mattered too. You could fail. You could be told no. And someone could stiff you.

Somewhere along the way, that lesson weakened.

Children now go door to door raising money for school programs that used to be budgeted. Municipal agencies solicit donations for services already funded by taxes. Universities and nonprofits run permanent fundraising campaigns, complete with legacy circles and planned giving strategies.

These institutions are not starving. Begging is baked in the cake, for all of them.

————

At the same time, our society has grown increasingly suspicious of the systems that actually produce surplus.

"Capitalism," "profit," and "private enterprise" are treated as moral failures by default, regardless of how wealth is created. The assumption is that accumulation itself is suspect. Property is theft, blah blah blah. (Well, other people's property, that is.)

Meanwhile, extraction—if framed correctly—is virtuous.

Universities do it. Municipal agencies do it. Nonprofits and NGOs do it. Public-sector unions do it. There are legacy circles, matching drives, estate solicitations. These institutions are not simply asking; they have built perpetual asking into their business model.

Occasionally, this slides from polite solicitation into outright grift. The Reverend Jackson model—"moral authority" converted into extortion in one form or another—has been replicated many times. The BLM episode is simply a modern, accelerated version: grievance becomes urgency, urgency becomes money, money disappears behind moral opacity.

The point isn't ideology. It's structure.

When asking becomes easier than producing, behavior follows.

————

This shift carries real societal consequences for all of us.

A society that normalizes cadging doesn't just weaken its economy; it erodes its people. Individuals raised in this environment are denied the dignity that comes from competence. Responsibility is externalized. Success is framed as exploitation, failure as injustice.

Psychologists call this learned helplessness. We are now a society of the learned helpless.

It produces fragility, resentment, and dependence—traits that are rewarded in the short term and corrosive in the long term. Victimhood becomes a valuable currency. Actual agency is now rather suspicious.

These are not harmless ideas.

Ideas shape behavior. Bad ideas don't merely mislead; they damage. Slowly at first, then all at once.

————

Risk Analysis, Not Nostalgia

This isn't nostalgia, and it isn't a glory days rant about "Well, in my day we learned to work at an early age . . . but kids these days . . ."

It's risk analysis for the general population.

What happens when more people seek income by claiming than by creating? What happens when work is shamed and dependency elevated?

We are running that experiment now.

Most of us appear not to notice.

To borrow from Bach: *Sleepers, awake.*

Chapter 3: George Orwell Requests a Court Time

Is the Eugene YMCA the New Minitrue?

Orwell's Newspeak, Tracktown Edition

There is a word the Eugene YMCA has been using for a while now to describe those of us who built the Tennis Center, funded it for nearly five decades, paid a premium membership every year, and showed up on volunteer days to paint and clean our facility. You may note that is something that no other YMCA member was ever asked to do with any of the YMCA's facilities—swimmers never were called to volunteer days to swab out the pool, the weight room crowd never gathered to wipe down the machines and the walls. But back to the tennis community who now have the temerity to object when the institution that promised to operate it as a tennis center has quietly decided to do something else, use it as a multi-activity big boxy thing.

And the word they use, well, it just sort of sticks in the craw, you know?

The word is *passionate*.

We are, according to the YMCA's official communications, a "passionate community." Our concerns are noted with faux warmth and something resembling institutional affection. Our objections are received with patience, the way a kindergarten teacher receives a child's declaration that recess has been cancelled unfairly. We have, one gathers, big feelings about things. Our big feelings are acknowledged. Our big feelings are respected. They are, in the Orwellian tradition, managed.

George Orwell, who knew something about the uses of language as a tool of power, would have recognized the move immediately. In his 1946 essay *Politics and the English Language*, he observed that the great enemy of clear language is insincerity — that when there is a gap between one's real aims and one's declared aims, one turns instinctively to vague, decorative words. Words that appear to say something while carefully avoiding the thing that needs to be said.

Passionate is one of those words.

What the YMCA means when it calls us passionate is, roughly, this: you are emotional, we are rational; you are attached, we are strategic; you are being selfish, we are generous; you are in the way, and we would prefer that you move. The word performs a quiet sleight of hand — it acknowledges our presence while dismissing our argument. It substitutes sentiment for substance. It implies that our objection is pretty much a feeling to be soothed, rather than a claim to be answered.

Our claim, to be plain about it, is simple: promises were made. We kept our promises for forty-five years. And now, to the Eugene Family YMCA, apparently, promises have become optional.

————

Down the YMCA Memory Hole

Orwell invented the Memory Hole for his novel *Nineteen Eighty-Four* — a slot in the wall of the Ministry of Truth into which inconvenient documents, photographs, and records were deposited and incinerated. The past, once altered, stayed altered. There was no appeal to what had actually happened, because what had actually happened no longer existed anywhere except in individual memory, which was unreliable. Which was the point.

I'm not accusing the Eugene YMCA of operating a literal Ministry of Truth. Eugene is not Airstrip One. The

stakes are considerably smaller, and the weather is
considerably wetter.

But consider the sequence of events at our Tennis
Center, and ask yourself whether Orwell's metaphor has
lost any of its edge.

The Tennis Center was built in the late 1970s by the
Eugene tennis community — funded by us, on YMCA
land, on the mutual understanding that the YMCA would
operate it as a tennis center in perpetuity. For more than
four decades, both sides kept that agreement. There may
or may not be documents. Community memory, the
building itself, and forty-five years of continuous
operation constitute their own form of evidence. The
evidence of a contract, as any lawyer knows, can be
established by conduct as much as by paper, especially if
the paper is lacking.

Then, as plans developed for a new YMCA facility, the
tennis community sought and received explicit
assurances: the Tennis Center would remain. Tennis
programming would continue. The historic relationship
would be honored. And, yes, indeed, the Y was very
happy to cash our contribution checks for the new
palatial digs.

Then things began to change. Gradually, then all at
once.

The first signal was linguistic. The Y renamed the
Tennis Center — quietly, without ceremony, without even
the courtesy of a by your leave — to incorporate
pickleball. This is worth pausing on. Orwell understood
that renaming is not a neutral administrative act. It is a
claim about reality going forward. To retitle the Tennis
Center is the first step to get to a place where it was
never purely a tennis center to begin with, that the
community that built it has no special claim upon it, and
that whatever understanding existed between that

community and the YMCA is now a matter of interpretation rather than obligation.

Control the name, and you begin to dissolve the history. Dissolve the history, and the obligation evaporates with it.

The pickleball lines were painted permanently over the tennis courts — the courts the tennis community had recently funded for resurfacing — again without any real conversation. The longtime tennis director and others, decades of accumulated coaching expertise, were dismissed. Members who complained about the new direction were, in some cases, told to seek tennis elsewhere. At the private club, specifically. The one the Tennis Center was built, in part, to provide an alternative to.

My goodness, we are a small town, but we seem to be creating our own little epic tale, aren't we? The Iliad, the Aeneid, the Milagro Bean Field War, step aside. I give you: The Tennis Center Affair. Will it have legs?

And then there is the plaque.

————

The Plaque

For years, a small, modest plaque hung in the Tennis Center honoring the original donors — the people who conceived the facility, raised the money, and built it. Nothing fancy; exactly the kind of understated marker that self-effacing community builders of the 1970s would have chosen. They built the thing, put up a quiet acknowledgment, and got back to playing tennis. The plaque was not prominently displayed. It had been moved, at some point, to the bathroom area, which is the institutional equivalent of a polite demotion. Not gone, exactly, but not celebrated either. Visible enough to satisfy a minimal obligation, obscure enough to avoid inconvenient questions.

And then it disappeared entirely.

I want to be precise here, because precision matters when making claims. The plaque is gone. Whether it was removed deliberately, misplaced in the move to the new facility, or simply lost in the shuffle of institutional change, I can't say with certainty. What I can say is that it is gone, it has been gone for a long time, and that its absence is not a small thing.

A plaque honoring the founders of a community-built facility is not decoration. It is a record, and it says: these people did this thing for our benefit, and it mattered, and we remember.

The plaque's removal — whether deliberate or negligent — sends the opposite message. It says the record has been revised. The founders have been de-recognized. The building, going forward, has no particular foundation story that anyone should remember or honor.

In Orwell's Ministry of Truth, this would be called rectification. The historical record has now been updated to reflect current institutional needs.

In Eugene, Oregon, we call it losing a plaque. Which sounds smaller. Which is, perhaps, the point.

————

What *Passionate* Really Means

There is a meeting scheduled for February 25, 2026, at which the future of the Tennis Center will be discussed. The tennis community will attend. We will be described, in all likelihood, as passionate.

We are, in fact, something more specific than that. We are, in fact, pissed off. We are pissed off people who built something, kept our word, relied on the word of an institution we trusted, and are now watching that institution rewrite the terms of a forty-five-year agreement without our consent and without the honesty to say plainly what it is doing.

Orwell's great insight was not that governments lie — everyone knew that — but that language is the mechanism by which lying becomes invisible, even to the liars themselves. When you call people passionate, you don't have to engage their argument. When you rename a building, you don't have to acknowledge what you've displaced. When you move a plaque to a bathroom and then lose it completely, you don't have to confront what the plaque represents.

The Tennis Center was built on an exchange of promises. The tennis community has kept its side of that exchange for nearly fifty years. The YMCA has recently stopped keeping its side, and has chosen to describe our objection to that fact as a matter of emotion rather than ethics.

Orwell would have found the whole thing depressingly familiar.

We find the fight worth fighting.

————

February 25

The YMCA has scheduled a community meeting for February 25 to discuss the future of the Tennis Center. The tennis community, understandably, would like to know what will be discussed.

We have been asking, politely. At least three long-standing tennis members — people who between them represent decades of membership, financial support, and institutional loyalty — have requested, over the course of approximately two months, some indication of the meeting's agenda or substance. They have been stonewalled. Completely, consistently, and apparently without embarrassment.

Interested community members have nonetheless been invited to attend and, one presumes, to hear whatever next steps the institution has decided it is ready to share. This is, we are told, transparency. We look forward to learning what that word means in this particular context.

In the meantime, this piece will be waiting for them when they arrive.

————

This is the first in a series examining the Eugene YMCA Tennis Center, the community that built it, and the institutional decisions now placing both at risk. The author is a thirty-year YMCA member, former board member, and former board president.

Chapter 4: Why (Y) Tennis?
The Cathedral and the Museum

My wife and I walked into the Eugene Family YMCA Tennis Center for the first time in 1995. We were not actually tennis players. We thought we might like to become tennis players, which is a different thing entirely. The difference is roughly the distance between thinking about a religion and actually having one.

Thirty years later, we are still there every week. Our son learned the game at the center after South Eugene ended his basketball dream — fourteen years old, the third best point guard candidate for a team with only two slots available. Within a couple of years, he was the district tennis champion competing at the state championships. Our grandson has already done two sets of group lessons. We are not yet sure he has the fever, but he has begun to angle for more lessons, which will have to fit in among piano, basketball, and soccer — the joy of being seven years old.

Our story is not unusual. It is, in fact, the whole point.

For people who don't play tennis, a tennis center can look like a large, well-lit steel building — a multipurpose shell that might just as easily house hay, heavy equipment, or recreational vehicles. The physical structure tells you nothing about its purpose. It tells you nothing about its soul.

And never doubt that a tennis center — every tennis center — has a soul. The same way the old YMCA building — the one that stood from 1952 to 2024 — had a soul, a profound one with a flat roof that leaked. A soul the new building on 24th Avenue is still actively searching for. I hope it will find one. But it takes years to build a soul, and very little time to destroy one.

What gives a tennis center its soul is not the building. It is the tennis brain and the tennis spirit inside it. Both of these come from the same source: a tennis director who understands the game, can play and teach it at a high level, and believes without qualification in the good of offering this sport to anyone from age one to ninety-two.

Remove the director, and you have a building. A nice building, perhaps. But a building.

The Museum

Jorge Luis Borges, who spent much of his life as a librarian and much of the rest thinking about what libraries mean, described entering one this way: "Leaving behind the babble of the plaza, I enter the Library. I feel, almost physically, the gravitation of the books, the enveloping serenity of order, time magically desiccated and preserved."

Time magically desiccated and preserved. That is what a sacred space does. It stops the clock not by freezing the present but by making the past continuously available — holding it in the room, in the air, in the accumulated meaning of everything that has happened there.

A tennis center is like a museum.

A museum costs money to build and survives because a specific community believes in its purpose. Measured against neighboring buildings—office buildings, shops and restaurants—that host thousands of visitors daily, a museum can appear woefully underused. Quiet, half empty. But every person who walks through a museum door comes with intent — to engage, to learn, to encounter something beyond the ordinary traffic of daily life.

Museum-goers do not have to be great artists to have a direct and somewhat mystical connection to great art.

They just have to show up with their eyes and minds open.

Tennis is the same. It is a museum-like connection, through time and space. You don't have to be Roger or Novak or Serena to feel their art and mastery, to understand in your body the geometry of a well-struck crosscourt backhand, to experience what it means to compete under pressure with nothing between you and the result except your own preparation and nerve. You just have to reserve a court time, show up, open a new can of balls, and bounce them a few times before you serve.

It would border on scandal for some group to appropriate thirty percent of a museum's square footage for thirty percent of the hours and hold paintball competitions or piñata tournaments. Imagine doing that — and then suggesting that the museum community was being selfish by not wanting to share.

The Cathedral

The historian of religion Mircea Eliade spent his career studying what distinguishes sacred space from ordinary space. His conclusion was precise: sacred space is "the really real" part of the universe, fixed and oriented, while profane space is ambiguous, without structure, without meaning. Sacred space is not merely special. It is the point from which everything else is oriented. Remove it, and the surrounding world loses its shape.

A cathedral exists not for efficiency but for enduring significance. It connects the present to the past, the local to the universal, the individual life to something larger than any single life can contain.

A tennis center — any tennis center — is a cathedral of movement, discipline, memory, and aspiration. It is a vessel for excellence, a place for character, a space

where generations meet and grow within the geometric
lines and established rules of a game that has been
played, on standardized surfaces with consistent
equipment, for centuries.

That continuity is not incidental. It is the point. When
you step onto a tennis court, you step into an unbroken
tradition that connects you — directly, through the
physics of the game itself — to every player who has ever
played it. The beginner and the grand slam champion are
playing the same game. The lines are in the same place.
The net is the same height. The rules have not changed.
There is a direct line, and you are on it.

Our tennis center introduced thousands of people to
that tradition, and welcomed thousands more across its
forty-five years. It has been a gift — not to a membership
demographic, not to a utilization metric, but to a
community. To families like mine. To futures that nobody
could have predicted in 1977 when Stan and Nate stood
in the rain and looked at a swampy lot and saw
something else.

Maybe you are getting the feeling this essay (means
"effort" by the way) is bouncing from topic to topic, kids
and grandkids, museums and cathedrals, trying to
describe a tennis center. Are there discrepancies,
contradictions? Maybe because a tennis center is like an
onion (there I go again), it's just layer after layer, all the
way down.

*"Do I contradict myself? Very well then I contradict
myself. I am large, I contain multitudes." — Walt
Whitman, Song of Myself*

Tennis contains multitudes. And so, perhaps, does
any honest essay about it.

The Martial Art

I want to say something about tennis that no one ever
said. Tennis is combat, *mano a mano.*

Tennis, played in whites on a warm summer evening, in the moonlight. I mean, *the very thought . . .*

Except, well, at its competitive level, tennis *is* a martial art.

Not metaphorically. Structurally. Like boxing, wrestling, judo, or karate, tennis pits one person directly against another, point after point, with nowhere to hide and no teammate to carry you. You hone your skills, practice your weapons. My old coach, Eric, called his baseline shots "hurt bombs." You can't call for a substitute in the third set, or sit down on the bench taking a breather while Coach Bob goes over his notes with you. You are out there on your own. Gladiator style. It is a physical contest, but also a contest of wills and of the mind. Strategy must be processed in real time, under fatigue, under pressure, in silence. At high school, collegiate, and USTA competitive levels, the demands on stamina, focus, and tactical thinking are extraordinary.

The critical difference from the martial arts is this: nobody gets hurt. An injury in tennis comes from poor technique, improper footwear, or a misstep — pilot error, not the sport itself. Tennis provides everything a martial art provides — the one-on-one contest, the mental pressure, the demand for discipline and preparation — without the collateral damage.

And, when it is over, the players shake hands.

That handshake is not a formality. It is the whole thing. It is the acknowledgment that what just happened between two people — the contest, the pressure, the small violences of competition — was conducted within agreed-upon rules, and that both players honored them, and that this matters. The handshake is civilization, compressed into a gesture.

It is a game executed mostly in silence except for the scoring, and ends, always, with a handshake, and a few almost whispered comments — because tennis is a quiet game, and the adjacent courts are still in full flow.

The 311 Years

The other day, on Court 2 at the Tennis Center, two players aged 87 and 85 played a full seventy-five-minute singles match.

On Court 1, two others aged 68 and 71 did the same.

Three hundred and eleven combined years of age. Two hundred and sixty-eight combined years of tennis experience, roughly. Self-regulating, always polite, each match ending with a handshake. A few quiet words. Then they gathered their things and left the courts for whoever had the next reservation.

Two days later, they were back. Every single week.

The 311 years played on, unaware that their sport had been determined to be underperforming.

What Is Being Lost

Decades of tennis coaching experience — the real software of any tennis facility — were dismissed summarily about two years ago. Players who wanted to improve, and young people who wanted to really learn the game, were told to go elsewhere. Some long-standing members, three and four decades at the center, who complained about the new direction, were told the same thing. Elsewhere, in Eugene, means the private club. The one the original tennis community built the Y center specifically so people wouldn't have to join.

The tennis center they built was not for the swells. It was for the forty-year-old who walks in out of the rain not yet knowing she needs this. It was for the kid whose first sport didn't work out and who finds, on a Tuesday afternoon on Court 3, that this one does. It was for the 85-year-old who will play a full singles match next Tuesday, and the Tuesday after that, until he can't.

We, the tennis community, share some of the fault for where we are. Unlike the founders, we have been way too passive — like the frog slowly boiling in the pot. Each change was absorbed with an *oh gosh* and a hope that it wouldn't be permanent.

It has become permanent unless we make it otherwise.

A museum without a curator is a warehouse. A tennis center without a tennis director, without the brain and the spirit that animate the building, is just a large, well-lit steel structure that could house almost anything at all.

Eliade wrote that you can't erase the past: "He cannot utterly abolish his past, since he himself is a product of his past. He forms himself by a series of denials and refusals, but he continues to be haunted by the realities that he has refused and denied."

The institution that now holds this building is an inheritor, a steward. It did not build what it now administers. Forty-five years of community trust, community investment, and community identity do not dissolve, unless we let it.

Chapter 5: Don Quijote, the Unicorn and the Tennis Center

Fifty-two years ago, in an apartment in Moncloa, I was reading *Don Quijote de la Mancha* in the original. I was a student at the Universidad de Madrid for a year, a serious student of Spanish by then—I had gone through several college courses of the Siglo de Oro, El Cantar de Mio Cid, Borges and the rest of the South American geniuses—and every afternoon I sat with Cervantes and a dictionary until my apartment-mate Anel came back from his classes for our chess matches. I was twenty years old and it took months. I would not trade a single hour of it.

The book is usually taught as a comedy about a man who has lost his mind. An old gentleman from La Mancha reads too many chivalric romances and decides he is a knight-errant. He sees giants where everyone else sees windmills. He sees a noble lady—his Dulcinea—where everyone else sees a common peasant woman (or, in Man of La Mancha, a scullery wench, a base prostitute). He sees enchantment and meaning and sacred purpose in a world that is, by every available measure, base, vulgar, and debased.

The joke, supposedly, is on him.

But Cervantes spent over a thousand pages on that joke, and by the end something significant has shifted. The people around Don Quijote—the ones who see the scullery wench and not Dulcinea, who see the windmill and not the giant, who measure the world by what is plainly and vulgarly in front of them—begin to seem not sensible but diminished. They are correct about everything and understand nothing. Don Quijote is wrong about the facts. But he may be the only one in the book who is paying attention to what the world is trying to tell him.

I think about Don Quijote these days more than I probably should. I think about him because I have spent the last two years trying to explain to a series of reasonable, well-meaning people that the thing they are holding is not a mere building to use as they please. And they keep showing me the spreadsheets and title records that prove it is.

*

My granddaughter Mira is five years old. She loves unicorns. This is standard-issue five-year-old behavior and I mention it only because her love of unicorns got me thinking.

I grew up the fourth of five boys in a quiet Protestant family in a Catholic suburb of Philadelphia. Fourth of five means you are not the oldest, who sets the standard, and not the youngest, who gets the exemption. You are the one nobody is keeping particular track of. A spare, in other words. There was nothing in our family ecosystem that could imagine a rainbow-colored horse in need of serious dental surgery. The word unicorn was never uttered in our house.

But watching Mira believe in impossible things with absolute conviction, I developed what I'll call—with full awareness of how it sounds—a Unicorn Theory of Phenomena. It has four axioms.

One: Real unicorns do not exist, never have, and never will.

Two: If you discover a real unicorn, cling to it. You will never find another.

Three: If you cling to the first unicorn, you will find more.

Four: If you find more, you will find yourself surrounded by, and walking among, unicorns every day.

The axioms contradict each other and they are all true. Axiom One? Well, isn't that just the world we have to deal with—a complete scarcity of unicorns. Axiom Two says, hold on tight because you'll never find another. Axiom Three says you will—but only because you grabbed the first one. The grabbing changes the odds. Belief, acted on, rearranges the world.

This is not mysticism. This is William James.

*

James—the American philosopher, Harvard psychologist, brother of the novelist, was a man who suffered enormously before he figured any of this out— wrote an essay in 1896 called "The Will to Believe." His argument, stripped to its core, was this: in certain situations, believing in something before you have proof is not irrational. It is the condition that makes the proof possible.

His examples were social. Whether a friendship will work depends on whether you trust the other person enough to act as though it will. Whether a community holds together depends on whether enough people believe it's worth holding together. The belief is not a response to the evidence. The belief is the evidence—the first piece of it, the one that makes all the other pieces fall into place.

That is Unicorn Axiom Three stated as philosophy. You cling to the first unicorn and more appear. Not because of magic, but because the act of commitment reorganizes your relationship to the world. You begin to see things you could not see before. You become available to things that could not reach you before. James would say: Of course. What did you expect? You finally made yourself present to the Universe.

In 1977, two men named Stan and Nate looked at a swampy lot in Eugene, Oregon—rain coming down, nothing there but mud and possibility—and believed that a community tennis center could rise from it. They had no proof it would work. They had no utilization study. They had a conviction that this sport—the one they loved so much—should be available to everyone, and that if they built the place, the community would come.

But then Eugene itself is a unicorn — a college town with somebody's first name, sitting where two gorgeous rivers meet, seventy miles from the ocean and seventy miles from the mountains, the kind of place that has always believed in things before the proof arrived. Stan and Nate fit right in.

William James would have recognized them instantly. They were acting on belief before the evidence arrived. They were wagering that the commitment would create its own justification.

It did. For forty-five years, it did.

*

What Stan and Nate's wager produced was not a membership base. It was a culture—the kind that takes decades to grow and cannot be replicated by intention. A place where a family could walk in knowing nothing about tennis and walk out, thirty years later, having built three generations of their lives around it. Where a fourteen-year-old whose first sport rejected him could find, on a Tuesday afternoon, that this one would not. Where a seven-year-old could take his first lessons in the same building where his grandmother still plays every week.

That is Axiom Three made flesh. The unicorn multiplied. Not because of a strategic plan but because of faithfulness—because when you protect something rare and keep showing up for it, it teaches other people how to show up too.

*

Now let us speak of Martin Buber, and about what is being done to the unicorn.

Buber was an Austrian-born Jewish philosopher who spent his life on a single question: what is the difference between truly encountering something and merely using it? His answer, published in 1923, divided all human experience into two modes. He called them I-Thou and I-It.

I-Thou is the mode of encounter. You meet something —a person, a place, a tradition—as a living presence. You do not measure it. You do not ask what it is for. You stand before it and recognize that it has a reality and a dignity that exist independent of your plans for it.

I-It is the mode of use. You look at the same person, the same place, the same tradition, and you see a resource. An object. Something to be managed, optimized, measured against a benchmark. I-It is not evil. You need it to run a budget, schedule a meeting, count the chairs. But when I-It is the only mode you have— when you look at a forty-five-year-old community institution and see nothing but square footage and hourly throughput—something has gone very wrong.

About two years ago, the institution that holds the Eugene YMCA Tennis Center looked at it in I-It mode and apparently did not like what it saw. The building was underperforming. Courts were not full at every hour. The tennis community, measured against the thousands of daily visitors to neighboring facilities, looked small. Quiet. Possibly dispensable.

So they optimized. The coaching—the accumulated knowledge that had turned beginners into players and players into a community for decades—was dismissed. Members who questioned the new direction were told to go elsewhere. Go elsewhere. In Eugene, elsewhere has only one meaning, and it costs what Stan and Nate built this center so nobody would have to pay.

Buber would have understood exactly what happened. The institution switched from I-Thou to I-It. It stopped encountering the tennis center and started measuring it. And because a unicorn cannot survive being measured—because the thing that made the building extraordinary was never the building, it was the life inside it—the unicorn began to die.

That is how you kill a unicorn, by the way. You don't have to be malicious. You just have to be efficient.

*

Back to Don Quijote.

There is a scene in the novel—and in the musical, which I have loved since I was young, long before I read the original—where the people around Don Quijote finally succeed in making him see "reason." They cure him of his delusions. He stops seeing giants. He stops seeing enchantment. He agrees that the world is base, vulgar, and debased, and that he was a fool to see it otherwise.

And then he dies.

Cervantes understood something that Buber would formalize three centuries later and that William James would frame as psychology: when you strip a life of its capacity to encounter the extraordinary, you have not made that life more rational. You have reduced it, made it less alive. Don Quijote, deluded and ridiculous and tilting at windmills, was more fully present in the world than every sensible person who tried to correct him.

I am not comparing myself to Don Quijote. I am not that far gone. Yet. But I will tell you this: I have spent two years trying to explain to reasonable people that our tennis center is not a building, and they keep looking at me the way the barber and the priest looked at the old knight—kindly, patiently, as though I am the one who has lost the plot.

The plot is a unicorn. I have not lost it.

I am trying to save it.

*

My grandson is seven, a first grader. I would like for him and all the other first graders to have a chance to catch tennis fever one day. The fever requires a place to catch it. It requires a building with life inside it—with coaching, with community, with the accumulated weight of decades of people who showed up and kept showing up.

You cannot catch the fever in a building that has been optimized. You cannot catch it from a utilization metric. You catch it from a person—a coach, a playing partner, a Tuesday regular who has been showing up longer than you've been alive—and that person is only there because somebody, forty-five years ago, believed in something that did not yet exist.

William James: the belief creates the conditions for its own proof.

Martin Buber: you must encounter it as a presence, not manage it as a thing.

Cervantes: the man who sees only what is plainly there will never see what matters.

And the Unicorn Theory: when you find something that is not supposed to exist, you hold on. It's the most important thing to cling to.

Chapter 6: Survey Says? GIGO.

A Tennis Family Feud, a Seventy-Five-Thousand-Dollar Permission Slip, and Why I Won't Fill Out the Questionnaire

"I would prefer not to." — Bartleby, in Herman Melville's "Bartleby, the Scrivener" (1853)

Oh the games people play now/every night and every day now / never meaning what they say now / and never saying what they mean. — Joe South, "Games People Play" (1969)

"Hey, Doug, are you filling out the Y's survey on the tennis center?"

"I'd rather have a root canal and a colonoscopy on the same day. In the same room. Performed by the same guy, maybe at the same time if he's an ambidextroid. At least that doctor would be honest about what he was looking for."

The Announcement

When the YMCA board announced that it was hiring a consultant—those guys who borrow your watch to tell you the time—to conduct a "comprehensive community needs assessment" for the tennis center area, it sounded like good governance. It sounded like listening. The board was going to spend seventy-five thousand dollars to bring in an independent firm, survey the community, analyze the data, and let the findings guide the future of a facility that mattered deeply to the people who used it. The tennis community—players, coaches, families who had built years of their lives around those courts—heard the announcement and felt, perhaps for the first time, that their voices might actually count.

They were wrong. The study was never designed to discover what the community needed. It was designed to produce a document that said the community needed exactly what the board had already decided to build. Nobody spends $75K without making sure they will get exactly what they are paying for.

The Decision That Preceded the Data

The redevelopment plan existed long before the consultant was retained. The broad strokes had been sketched in closed sessions, discussed among board leadership, and socialized with staff. The tennis center area represented valuable real estate—not in the commercial sense, but in the institutional sense. It was space that could be repurposed, reimagined, and used to justify capital campaigns and strategic vision statements. The board had plans for that space. What the board did not have was permission.

The tennis community was organized, vocal, and passionate. These were not casual users who would shrug and find another gym. They were people who had invested time—now 49 years—, money, and social capital in those courts. They had leagues, lessons, and traditions. They showed up at meetings. They wrote letters. They were, in the language of institutional politics, the main problem.

And so the board faced a familiar dilemma: how do you do what you have already decided to do when the people most affected by that decision are loudly opposed to it? The answer, refined by decades of nonprofit and corporate governance practice, is elegant in its cynicism. You do not argue with the opposition. You do not overrule them. You do not even acknowledge that a decision has been made. Instead, you announce a process. You hire an expert. You commission a study. And you let the study do the arguing for you.

The Covenant They Would Rather You Forgot

But the consultant study serves a deeper purpose than merely silencing opposition or providing bureaucratic cover. It is an end run around a knotty ethical problem that the board would prefer not to confront directly: the mutual promises made fifty years ago when the tennis center was created.

Facilities like this one do not materialize from institutional generosity alone. They are built on promises. Donors gave money because they were told it would support tennis. Members joined because tennis was part of the covenant. Families organized their lives to some degree around the facility because the Y, by word and deed, represented that the tennis center would be there for them. These were not casual understandings. They were the moral and, in many cases, legal foundations upon which the facility was built.

Livin' in a post-moral and post-virtue age

The philosopher Alasdair MacIntyre, in his landmark 1981 work *After Virtue*, argued that modern institutions have largely lost the capacity for genuine moral reasoning. They cannot make substantive ethical arguments because they have replaced moral discourse with procedural legitimacy. When an institution cannot defend a decision on its merits—when it cannot look the people it made promises to in the eye and explain why those promises no longer matter—it substitutes a process for an argument. The "community needs assessment" is that process. It allows the board to avoid the uncomfortable question—"Are we honoring the commitments we made when this facility was created?"—and replace it with a technocratic question that is far easier to answer in their favor: "What does the data say the community needs today?"

The shift is subtle but decisive. A question about promises is a moral question. It requires the board to grapple with obligation, trust, and the meaning of its word. A question about community needs is a management question. It requires only a survey and a spreadsheet. By commissioning the study, the board has moved the conversation from ethics to analytics—from a courtroom where they might lose to a conference room where the consultant has already arranged the furniture.

The Law of Broken Promises

The board's desire to sidestep the promise question is not merely a matter of institutional comfort. There is a legal dimension they would rather not test. Donor restrictions on charitable gifts are not advisory. They are binding legal obligations, and the law provides remedies when nonprofits violate them.

The landmark case is *Robertson v. Princeton University*. In 1961, Marie and Charles Robertson gave Princeton $35 million—then the largest single gift to any university—restricted to training students for government service. Over the ensuing decades, Princeton drifted from that purpose, using the funds (which had grown to roughly $900 million) for programs the Robertsons never intended. In 2002, the family sued. The six-year litigation ended in a settlement in which Princeton paid approximately $100 million—$40 million in legal fee reimbursement and $50 million plus interest to fund a new foundation carrying on the donors' original mission. It remains the largest financial award in the history of donor intent litigation.

Equally instructive is *Smithers v. St. Luke's-Roosevelt Hospital Center*, decided by a New York appellate court in 2001. R. Brinkley Smithers gave $10 million to establish an alcoholism treatment center in a dedicated facility. After his death, the hospital announced plans to sell the building, relocate the program, and divert the proceeds. The donor's widow discovered the hospital had been transferring endowment funds to its general account. The court ruled that the donor's estate had standing to enforce the gift terms, holding that the donor of a charitable gift is in a better position than the Attorney General to be vigilant and to enforce his or her own intent. The court granted a preliminary injunction blocking the hospital from disbursing the sale proceeds.

These cases establish a clear principle: when a nonprofit accepts money, support, or participation on the basis of specific commitments, those commitments have legal force. The legal path to modifying a fifty-year-old commitment runs through a courtroom and a doctrine called cy pres—which requires the modification to be as close as possible to the donor's original intent—not through a community needs assessment designed to make the question disappear.

Hiring the Verdict

The selection of the consulting firm is where the outcome is quietly pre-determined. In a legitimate needs assessment, the board would define a genuinely open question—what does this community need from this space?—and invite a firm to investigate it without preconditions. That is not what happens in the captive board model. The scope of work is crafted, by staff aligned with the redevelopment plan, to frame the question in a way that makes only one answer possible. The firm is briefed on the institution's "strategic direction." The fix is in. "We hired an independent outside firm. We spent seventy-five thousand dollars on a rigorous, data-driven analysis. We followed the process." This is the language of liability management, not governance. It is designed to survive a deposition, not to produce the best outcome for the community.

The French sociologist Jacques Ellul saw this coming. In his 1962 work *Propaganda: The Formation of Men's Attitudes*, Ellul argued that the most effective propaganda is never the crude lie. Far more dangerous is what Ellul called integration propaganda—the use of real data, selectively gathered and carefully framed, to lead the audience to a conclusion that appears to have emerged organically from the evidence itself. The propagandist does not fabricate. He curates. He chooses which questions to ask, which populations to survey, which benchmarks to use, which trends to emphasize. The data is real. The analysis, within its defined parameters, is real. What is artificial is the frame—and the frame is everything.

This is the art of the managed study. Computer scientists have a term for this: GIGO—Garbage In, Garbage Out. Design the inputs to guarantee the outputs. If you survey a broad population about broad preferences, you will get broad answers. If you frame every question around the redevelopment and exclude the option of keeping the tennis center, the data will discover that the community wants the redevelopment. The garbage is not in the data. The garbage is in the question.

Exhibit A: The Questionnaire

Noam Chomsky and Edward Herman, in *Manufacturing Consent* (1988), described a process they called the narrowing of the bounds of acceptable debate. The most effective form of ideological control, they argued, is not censorship but the careful management of which questions get asked. Once the frame is set, vigorous debate can proceed within it—and the appearance of robust debate reinforces the legitimacy of the frame.

The Y's consultant questionnaire is a textbook application of this principle. Consider the actual questions being put to the community:

The following question pertains to new construction at the Y's property on Patterson Street, adjacent to the existing Tennis & Pickleball Center. The vision for this new construction is to help the Y expand its ability to address youth development, healthy living and social responsibility needs. A central component is the construction of 4 large 1,600 sq. ft (each) multi-purpose rooms. Please choose your top 3 most important needs for the YMCA to offer in these multi-purpose rooms.

Notice what this question does. The new construction is presented as a fait accompli—not "should the Y build," but "what should go inside the building the Y has already decided to build." The "vision" is stated as settled fact. Every option is a non-tennis activity. Tennis is not a choice. The respondent is being asked to pick the color of the coffin.

In addition to the 4 large multi-purpose rooms, what else should the YMCA consider in the new development adjacent to the current Tennis & Pickleball Center at the Patterson Campus? Please choose your top 2.

The same technique, applied again. Recovery suites, co-working spaces, foosball tables—the options read like a WeWork brochure. No option says "invest in the existing tennis facility." The question does not permit that answer.

The YMCA would like to ensure that its 27,000 square foot indoor facility that was opened in the 1970s to serve the community's tennis needs, and later updated to also meet pickleball needs, is being utilized to meet the highest community needs and having the greatest impact.

This is the cruelest question, and the most revealing. The facility "was opened in the 1970s to serve the community's tennis needs"—past tense, historical framing, as if tennis is a relic of the disco era. The phrase "later updated to also meet pickleball needs" is doing especially cynical work: the conversion of tennis court time to pickleball—which many in the tennis community experienced as a deliberate campaign to push them out— is recast as a generous modernization. And then the thesis statement, dressed as a neutral prompt: the Y wants to ensure the space "is being utilized to meet the highest community needs and having the greatest impact." This presupposes that tennis is not the highest need, and invites you to rank what should replace it.

What is missing from every question is what matters most. No question asks: "Should the tennis center remain a tennis center?" No question asks: "Is the Y honoring its fiduciary duty of stewardship to the donors who built this facility?" No question acknowledges that commitments were made, that donors gave money for tennis, that members joined for tennis, that a community organized itself around a promise. You are free to argue about yoga versus Pilates, cold therapy versus steam rooms, foosball versus ping pong. You are not free to argue that a promise should be kept.

The Wrong Metric

The consultant's report will almost certainly frame the tennis center as underperforming. It will measure tennis usage as a percentage of total YMCA membership and conclude that the facility serves a small fraction of the community. It will present utilization data showing hours when courts are not fully booked and call this inefficiency. This is the wrong metric, and the people writing the scope of work know it.

Even putting aside all of the aggressive actions the Y has taken to disrupt and downgrade tennis qua tennis— firing all the tennis staff and hiring people who de facto know nothing about it, defacing the newly surfaced courts, the incredible noise pollution and disruption of putting 16 or more pickleballers 4 feet away from a singles court, changing up playing times and creating ersatz programming—the right questions about the tennis center are simple. Is the facility paid off? Are the tennis memberships fully subscribed? Are those memberships covering maintenance costs, staffing, and operations? Can the tennis community, as it exists today, afford real tennis directors and professional staff? If the answers are yes—and in a fifty-year-old facility with a committed membership base, they very likely are—then the tennis center is not a problem to be solved. It is an asset to be celebrated.

No gym evaluates its performance the way this consultant will evaluate the tennis center. Every gym in America knows the resolution effect: three hundred people sign up in January with good intentions, the facility is packed through February, and by May the crowds have thinned to the committed core who show up year-round. Tennis does not have a resolution effect. Tennis has committed, year-round, paying members who show up in February and August alike—members who book courts, take lessons, play leagues, and renew their memberships because the facility is woven into their lives.

The multi-purpose rooms the board wants to build will follow the resolution curve. They will be packed in January with people who signed up for yoga and HIIT classes, half-empty by Memorial Day, and requiring new programming, new marketing, and new fundraising campaigns to fill the space again. The tennis center does not have this problem. But the consultant will not frame the comparison this way, because the scope of work was not written to ask whether the existing facility is financially self-sustaining. It was written to ask what should replace it.

The Questions That Matter

If the consultant's study were a genuine inquiry, the questionnaire would look very different. And if you are a member of this YMCA, these are the questions you should be asking—of the consultant, of the board, loudly, and in public:

Is the tennis center paid off, and are its memberships covering its costs? If tennis memberships are fully subscribed and covering maintenance, staffing, and operations, then the board is not proposing to fix a problem. It is proposing to destroy a functioning asset and replace it with one that will require twelve million dollars in capital and perpetual fundraising to sustain.

Should the Y honor its ethical, legal, and reputational obligations to the tennis donors and the tennis community? This is the threshold question—the one that must be answered before any discussion of redevelopment can proceed in good faith.

Should the Y launch yet another cadging, begging capital campaign—or build a YMCA Tennis Academy that puts it on the map? The redevelopment plan envisions a facility that will compete with every private gym, daycare, and yoga studio in the area—a market already saturated—while requiring perpetual fundraising to sustain.

Who controls the process? Who selected the consulting firm? Who defined the scope of work? Was it written to include the possibility that the current use is the best use? Who provided the data? Does the scope require the consultant to evaluate the Y's legal obligations to the donors who created the tennis center? Will the board release the full report, including raw survey data and methodology, before any vote?

The board's willingness or unwillingness to answer these questions will tell you everything you need to know about whether the study is a genuine inquiry or a hundred-thousand-dollar permission slip.

Why I Will Not Fill Out the Questionnaire

In 1853, Herman Melville published "Bartleby, the Scrivener: A Story of Wall Street," in which a copyist in a law office, asked to perform one routine task after another, responds each time with the same quiet, devastating phrase: "I would prefer not to." Bartleby does not argue. He does not explain. He does not engage with the premises of the request. He simply declines—politely, immovably, and without apology.

The YMCA has asked the community to respond to this questionnaire as part of the consultant's study. I would prefer not to.

I am not declining because I am indifferent to the outcome. I am declining because participating would lend legitimacy to a process designed to produce a predetermined result. Every completed survey becomes a data point when reporting that hundreds or thousands of community members participated in a comprehensive assessment. My participation becomes evidence that the process was open and inclusive—even if the questions were framed to yield only one conclusion. We shouldn't contribute to some Kabuki theater of our own disenfranchisement.

Vaclav Havel, the Czech playwright and dissident who would later become his country's president, described this dynamic in his 1978 essay "The Power of the Powerless." Havel tells the story of a greengrocer in communist Czechoslovakia who places a Party slogan —"Workers of the World, Unite!"—in his shop window. The greengrocer does not believe the slogan. He displays it because compliance is the price of being left in peace.

Filling out the Y's questionnaire is putting the sign in the window. It says: I accept the premise. I agree that a survey is the right way to continue decimating a fifty-year-old promise. I consent to having my concerns about institutional integrity diluted into a data set alongside the preferences of people who have never set foot on the tennis courts and have no knowledge of the commitments that created them.

And then comes the moment Havel describes: the day the greengrocer stops putting up the sign. He stops voting in elections he knows are a farce. He begins to say what he really thinks.

My refusal to participate is a small act. But it rests on a principle Havel articulated and that applies here: participation is never neutral. In a process designed to produce a predetermined conclusion, compliance is complicity. The only honest response to a rigged question is to refuse to answer it—and to say, clearly and publicly, why.

Any good securities trader knows the phrase, "No position is also a position." So, call my non-participation in this farce a vote of no confidence.

The question I want answered is not on the questionnaire. The question I want answered is: Does the YMCA intend to honor the commitments it made when the tennis center was created? If the answer is yes, the study is unnecessary. If the answer is no, the study is a cover story. In neither case is my participation useful to anyone except the people who need my name on their list of respondents.

A Pattern, Not an Anomaly

If this were happening at one YMCA, it might be an aberration. It is happening everywhere.

In Arlington, Virginia, the YMCA planned to tear down its facility and build a new recreation center

alongside a seven-story, 374-unit apartment building.
Tennis players watched the eight existing indoor courts—
the last public indoor courts in Arlington—get cut in half
in the plans, then eliminated entirely. In Brentwood,
Tennessee, the YMCA sold its Maryland Farms property
and discontinued one of Middle Tennessee's most
significant tennis operations—21 courts, a thriving junior
program, annual USTA tournaments—without offering a
transition plan. In Muncie, Indiana, the YMCA announced
a new consolidated facility and noted, almost as an
afterthought, that it would not include tennis courts.

The pattern is consistent. Tennis programs are
eliminated not because they are failing but because they
occupy space that institutional leadership has decided to
repurpose. The community that built and sustained the
program is treated as an obstacle to be managed rather
than a constituency to be served.

Seventy-Five Thousand Dollars' Worth of Nothing

The money is what lingers. Seventy-five thousand
dollars—donated by members, raised through campaigns,
earned through program fees—spent not on equipment,
not on coaching, not on scholarships or facility
improvements, but on a document whose primary
function is to protect the people who commissioned it
and to gaslight those opposed.

MacIntyre's diagnosis holds. The YMCA board cannot
make a moral case for breaking the promises that
created the tennis center. And so it does what
MacIntyre's emotivists always do: it replaces the moral
question with a managerial one, and it hires a consultant
to answer the managerial question in a way that makes
the moral question disappear.

There is another path. The board could have looked
at what it had—a thriving tennis community, a fifty-year
legacy, a facility with a story—and asked how to make it

extraordinary. A YMCA Tennis Academy—my proposal—
would have put this institution and its leadership on the
national map.

Instead, the board chooses to become another
generic Y: daycare, fitness classes, recovery suites, co-
working spaces—every one of them available from a
dozen competitors within a five-mile radius. And it spent
seventy-five thousand dollars on a consultant's report to
make this unimaginative, promise-breaking, financially
precarious decision look like the product of rigorous,
data-driven analysis.

The tennis players will lose their courts, eventually.
The board will approve the redevelopment. The
consultant will deposit the fee and move on to the next
engagement. And somewhere in the minutes of a board
meeting, in language polished to a bureaucratic shine,
there will be a sentence that reads something like:
"Following a comprehensive community needs
assessment conducted by an independent outside firm,
the board voted to proceed with the strategic
redevelopment of the tennis center area, consistent with
the consultant's data-driven recommendations."

Every word of that sentence is technically true. And
every word of it is a lie.

Chapter 7: Uncle Lou and the Smell in the Room

Every family has an Uncle Lou.

Uncle Lou is a lovely man. Kind, generous, wouldn't hurt a fly. Shows up to every Thanksgiving, every birthday, every Sunday dinner. Brings wine. Plays with the kids. Tells stories that are genuinely funny the first three times and endurable forever after because he is Uncle Lou and you are polite.

Uncle Lou has terrible breath and even worse body odor.

It is not his fault. Brushing his teeth does not help. Bathing does not help. Cologne makes it worse—now it's body odor wearing a disguise, which is more alarming than the original. It is just who he is. There is no malice in it. There is no solution to it. It is a condition, and the family has learned to live with it the way families learn to live with things: by opening windows, by angling their chairs, by breathing through their mouths during the long goodbye hug.

Uncle Lou, for his part, has no idea. He is nose-blind. He cannot smell what everyone else in the room can smell, because he has been living with himself his whole life. If you told him—and you would never tell him, because he is kind and you are not cruel—he would be genuinely hurt. He would not understand. He would say: but I showered this morning.

This essay is about pickleball, and I want to be as kind to pickleball as the family is to Uncle Lou. But someone needs to say what the room smells like.

*

The smell of pickleball is noise.

Not metaphorical noise. Not the kind of noise you can get used to, the way you get used to traffic or the hum of an appliance. Pickleball noise is a sharp, percussive, relentless crack—a hard polymer ball hitting a hard polymer paddle—repeated every two to three seconds, continuously, for the duration of play. It echoes off walls. It bounces off ceilings. It penetrates closed doors, insulated barriers, and the kind of mental concentration that tennis requires and that once was possible in this building.

R. Murray Schafer, the Canadian composer and acoustic ecologist who essentially invented the study of soundscapes, argued in his landmark 1977 book *The Soundscape* that unwanted noise is not merely unpleasant. It is a form of territorial aggression. Sound colonizes space the way an invasive species colonizes an ecosystem. The organism making the noise claims the territory; every other organism either adapts or leaves.

The crack of a pickleball paddle is one of the most acoustically aggressive sounds in recreational sports. It has been measured at 70 to 85 decibels at the source and remains clearly audible at distances well beyond the court. For context, a normal conversation is about 60 decibels. A tennis ball striking a racket is 40 to 50. The difference is not small. Decibels are logarithmic—every 10-decibel increase represents a doubling of perceived loudness. Pickleball is not a little louder than tennis. It is dramatically, structurally, inescapably louder. The pickleballers do not hear it. They are Uncle Lou. They have been living inside the sound for so long that it has become invisible to them.

*

But the smell is not only noise. The smell is also space.

Edward T. Hall, the American anthropologist who coined the term proxemics—the study of how humans use and share physical space—argued in *The Hidden Dimension (1966)* that every activity has what he called a spatial and acoustic envelope. The envelope is the total territory that an activity requires, including not just the physical footprint but the sound, the movement patterns, and the psychological space needed for the activity to function.

A tennis court's envelope is large physically—78 feet long, 36 feet wide, plus margins for overruns—but quiet acoustically. The sound of tennis is the brief pop of a ball, the squeak of a shoe, the occasional call of a score. It does not fill a building. Two people can play tennis on adjacent courts and barely be aware of each other.

A pickleball court's envelope is small physically—44 feet by 20 feet—but enormous acoustically. The crack fills a gym. It fills adjacent rooms. It fills the lobby. You can fit four pickleball courts in the space of one tennis court, which looks like efficiency on a spreadsheet and is a catastrophe in lived experience, because you have just quadrupled the acoustic envelope inside the same walls.

When two incompatible envelopes occupy the same building, Hall observed, the larger envelope displaces the smaller one. Not through conflict. Not through anyone's intention. Through physics. The louder activity makes the quieter activity impossible, the way a brass band makes a string quartet impossible even if the brass players are perfectly nice people who sincerely wish the violinists well.

Imagine getting a third of the space in a ballet academy and, while lessons and rehearsals are going on, bringing in a group of *Macarena* enthusiasts to practice. Or putting *foosball* tables in the reading room at the library. Or—and this is the one that comes closest— putting a batting cage inside a yoga studio. The batting cage people are having a great time. The yoga people can no longer function. Nobody is wrong. The activities are simply incompatible in the same space, and pretending otherwise is not diplomacy. It is delusion.

*

In 1968, the ecologist Garrett Hardin published an essay in Science called "The Tragedy of the Commons." It became one of the most cited papers in the history of the social sciences, and it describes exactly what is happening at the tennis center.

Hardin's argument is simple. When a shared resource —a commons—is open to multiple uses without management, the most aggressive use will destroy it for everyone. Not through malice. Through the logic of each user acting rationally within their own interest. The herder who adds one more cow to the common pasture is acting rationally. But when every herder adds one more cow, the pasture is destroyed. Nobody intended that outcome. The system produced it.

The tennis center is a commons. It has been a tennis commons for decades—a shared space where the activity and the space and the acoustic envelope were all calibrated to each other. The building was designed for tennis. The culture was built around tennis. The community that uses it and loves it and has invested three hundred years of combined playing time on Court 2 exists because the commons was managed for a purpose.

Introducing pickleball into that commons is adding a new cow to the pasture. The cow is not evil. The cow is just hungry. But the cow's appetite—the acoustic appetite, the spatial appetite, the scheduling appetite—is large enough to degrade the pasture for every other animal on it.

The tragedy of the commons is not that someone did something wrong. The tragedy is that nobody managed the commons, and the unmanaged commons collapsed under the weight of incompatible demands.

*

Here is the thing about Uncle Lou that the family has figured out but the Y has not.

You do not solve the Uncle Lou problem by putting him in the living room and asking everyone else to adapt. You solve it by not inviting Uncle Lou to dinner. You wish him well. You bear him no ill will. You do not poison his dog or slash his tires. But you do not sacrifice every family gathering to accommodate a condition that is his, not yours. If Uncle Lou wants to have people over at his own house, where his smell is his own business, then God bless him.

Pickleball is an outdoor sport. It was invented as a backyard game in 1965 on Bainbridge Island, about three hours north of here. It was played on driveways and patios for decades before anyone thought to bring it inside. And outside is where it belongs—the crack of the paddle dissipates in open air, and nobody has to share walls with it. The problem is not the people who play pickleball. The problem is the enclosure.

Dedicated outdoor pickleball courts are being built all over the country. They are relatively cheap to construct. They solve the noise problem by not having walls. They solve the space problem by not taking courts from another sport. They solve the commons problem by creating a separate commons. This is not complicated. This is Uncle Lou's own house.

But the Y has chosen to put Uncle Lou in the living room. And now the living room smells like Uncle Lou, and the family is being told to adapt.

*

One more thing, and it involves speculation about motives, which I have tried to avoid in these essays. But the fact is this: nobody in the tennis community believes that pickleball is the point.

The community's working theory is that pickleball is a stalking horse. In the old hunting sense: the thing the hunter walks behind while approaching his real target. The tennis community watches the horse—argues about

52

the horse, complains about the noise the horse makes—
while the hunter gets closer and closer.

The real target is the building, or the land, or
whatever the Y's redevelopment plans require. Pickleball
does not win in this scenario. Pickleball is the tool. The
tennis community is driven out by the noise and the
scheduling and the indignity of sharing a purpose-built
facility with an incompatible use. Then the pickleball
community, smaller and less attached to the building, is
easy to relocate or dissolve. And then the Y has an empty
building and a valuable piece of land and no community
organized enough to object to whatever comes next.

I do not know if this theory is correct. But the Y's
communications have done nothing to dispel it. Telling
the tennis community that their facility was "updated to
meet pickleball needs"—while the tennis community
experienced that update as a hostile invasion—is not
transparency. It is institutional gaslighting: they redescribe your experience until you doubt your own
memory.

If the Y's intentions are good—if they genuinely
believe that pickleball and tennis can coexist in the same
building—then they should welcome this conversation,
because the science and the acoustics and the spatial
analysis all point in one direction: build outdoor
pickleball courts, keep the tennis center for tennis, and
let both communities thrive in spaces designed for their
sports.

That is Uncle Lou's own house. That is the solution
the family has always known.

*

Uncle Lou is a perfectly nice man. We wish him well.

But he needs his own house. And we need our living
room back.

Chapter 8: The Palace on 24th Avenue

"While capitalism has a visible cost — profit — socialism has an invisible cost — inefficiency." — Thomas Sowell, Basic Economics

There is a new YMCA in Eugene, Oregon.

It opened in December 2023 at the corner of 24th and Hilyard, on the former site of Roosevelt Middle School. It is large, modern, and genuinely beautiful — warm-water therapy pool, lap pool, full gymnasium, youth development spaces, the works. The CEO called it "a gift to the community for the next hundred years."

He was not wrong about the gift part.

The building cost $48 million. Almost none of it was earned.

There is another YMCA facility in Eugene, older and smaller, that was entirely earned—built in 1979 by thirty-six community members who wrote checks and swung hammers. Its story is the photographic negative of this one, and we will get to it. But first, Le Palace.

*

Let me explain the difference between the two, because the distinction matters.

When a private developer builds a $48 million project, he has to have a plan when he goes to the bank. The bank will require him to have thought through his production, operations, sales and other input costs and reasonably predict enough revenue to service whatever mortgage and unsecured lending package they might approve. The actual market for the developer's product is indifferent to his intentions. If he prices his product too low, he fails. If he prices it too high, people go elsewhere. His operation either pays for itself or it doesn't, and if it doesn't, someone loses something real.

The Eugene YMCA operates under a different financial philosophy.

Of the $48 million: $15 million came from Oregon state lottery-backed bonds, authorized in House Bill 5030. Another $2 million arrived as a federal congressional earmark, inserted by Senator Merkley into the 2023 omnibus spending bill. The land — 5.42 acres of former school property — was purchased from the 4J school district over six years for $2.85 million. Corporate donors received naming rights in exchange for checks. And a network of individual "major donors" contributed in exchange for the social immortality that comes from having your family name attached to a warm-water therapy pool.

None of this is illegal. Most of it is tax-deductible. And as a 501(c)(3), the YMCA pays no federal income tax, no Oregon state income tax, and no property tax on its $55 million in assets. It is, in the fullest sense, a tax-free enterprise competing against taxpaying ones.

*

In my first piece on cadge creep, I described its street-level version: the teenager with a clipboard, the parks foundation soliciting donations for services already funded by taxes, the neighbor who gave forty dollars to a boy who may or may not have gone to London.

The YMCA is the same thing in a hard hat and a capital campaign.

The vocabulary is identical, just elevated. "Donors" instead of strangers. "Campaign" instead of drive. "Legacy circle" instead of clipboard. "Planned giving" instead of "remember us in your will." "Community partners" instead of marks. The moral architecture is the same: if you decline, you are against children, against health, against the community.

The Eugene YMCA employs a Chief Development Officer. They run matching campaigns with challenge donations. They have CRM systems tracking donor wealth and engagement. They retained professional fundraising consultants — $36,000 in fees in fiscal year 2024 alone, just for operations, on top of the six-figure consultants who ran the capital campaign.

One thing I find myself idly curious about: what fraction of the YMCA's total operating cost is actually devoted to the perpetual work of asking? The $36,000 in outside fundraising fees is only the visible tip. There is the Chief Development Officer at roughly $110,000 in salary plus benefits. Against that, they raised $1.6 million in contributions in fiscal year 2024. In a $48 million gleaming palace, built entirely on other people's money, they are losing approximately one dollar for every dollar they spend on fundraising.

The teenager with the clipboard has gone to business school.

*

Now for the part that Alexis de Tocqueville would have recognized immediately.

In 1835, Tocqueville wrote his Memoir on Pauperism, a text almost nobody reads anymore. He had noticed a paradox: England, the wealthiest country in Europe, had the most beggars. One-sixth of the kingdom, he calculated, lived at public expense. His diagnosis was precise: any institution that puts charity on a permanent administrative footing creates, inevitably, a class that lives at the expense of those who work. The institution designed to relieve poverty industrializes it instead.

The Eugene YMCA is not a poverty program. But the structural logic is identical.

You give an organization a $48 million building, tax-free. You exempt it from property taxes, income taxes, and taxes on investment income. You allow donors to deduct their gifts. You fund it with lottery bonds and congressional earmarks. At that point, the organization owns a $48 million asset with no debt and no cost of capital. By any reasonable standard — a 6% annual return on asset value is conservative — it should generate $3 million per year in operating surplus. Permanently. Without ever asking for another dollar.

Instead, in fiscal year 2024 — its first full year in the palace — the Eugene Family YMCA generated $9.08 million in revenue and spent $9.3 million. Net loss: $219,762. Total liabilities grew by roughly $3 million in a single year.

The gap between what this organization should produce and what it actually produces is approximately $3.2 million annually. And it is growing.

This is not a startup. This is an organization that received a gift and is still losing ground.

*

Here is where it gets interesting.

The YMCA's published rack rates, after their October 2024 rate increase, run from $32 per month for a youth membership to $73 per month for an adult — family plans up to $131. Blended across membership categories, call it $52 a month as a reasonable average sticker price.

The actual average yield per member is something else entirely.

Fiscal year 2024 program revenues were approximately $7.25 million, serving roughly 18,000 members. Allocate roughly half of that to membership dues — the other half being daycare, camps, lessons, and activity fees — and you get something in the range of $200 per person per year. Sixteen dollars and sixty-seven cents a month.

The blended rack rate is $52. The realized average is $16.67. The difference — $35 per member per month — is not a subsidy that gets filled in from somewhere else. It is simply revenue the YMCA chose not to collect. A voluntary pricing decision made possible only because someone else already paid for the building.

For context on what the market actually bears: two miles away, Planet Fitness charges maybe $15 a month. They pay property taxes, income taxes, and built their own facility. The Downtown Athletic Club — Eugene's 40-year-old, locally owned, full-service club with two pools, racquetball, squash, steam rooms and 60 fitness classes a week — charges $138 to $164 a month. They built their own building. They have always paid their own way.

*

There is something else worth naming about the membership growth.

The YMCA reports growing from roughly 4,000 members before the capital campaign to approximately 18,000-20,000 members after opening. This is presented as success. It may be. But membership doesn't arise from nothing.

Eugene's population is roughly 175,000. When the YMCA quintuples its membership at a realized price of $16.67 a month, some of those new members came from somewhere — gyms and studios that pay taxes, carry mortgages, and price their services to cover their costs without lottery bonds or congressional earmarks.

Thomas Sowell noted that profits are the price paid for efficiency — the invisible discipline that weeds out what doesn't work. Eliminate profit, and you eliminate the signal. The YMCA has no profit requirement. It has a donor development office instead.

*

One final irony, and then I'll let the building speak for itself.

The nonprofit sector — the YMCA very much included — tends toward a cultural politics that is skeptical of capitalism, suspicious of profit, and sympathetic to redistribution. This is fine; people are entitled to their views.

58

What is less fine is running a capital campaign like a Goldman Sachs roadshow while simultaneously deploring the system that makes capital campaigns comprehensible.

Milton Friedman noticed this tendency. The era of "unrestrained capitalism" that the sector deplores was, he pointed out, precisely the era when private charitable activity boomed — when Carnegie built his libraries, when colleges were founded across the country, when the original YMCA movement spread, all without tax deductions, lottery bonds, or congressional earmarks.

The Cadge Society replaced that system with something more elaborate, more professional, and, as the fiscal year 2024 numbers suggest, considerably less efficient.

*

Sowell's invisible cost—inefficiency—is not evenly distributed. It has to come from somewhere. In the Eugene YMCA system, we now know exactly where.

The Tennis Center is the oldest continuously operating program asset in the Eugene YMCA system — built in 1979 by thirty-six community members who wrote checks and swung hammers, entrusted to the Y on a handshake, and self-sustaining for forty-five years.

The Y's director has reportedly described the Tennis Center as "cash positive" — as long as you do not count the cost of the people required to run it. This is a remarkable sentence, and it deserves a moment of quiet appreciation. The Tennis Center is profitable if you exclude its expenses. By that logic, every business in America is profitable. Manuel's taco truck is a gold mine if you don't count the tacos.

The actual math: a director at $60,000, staff coverage of roughly 200 hours per week at $20 an hour — call it $192,000 annualized — plus a conservative 20% employer burden, brings total staffing cost to approximately $302,000. Against that, revenue from a membership that has declined from 500 to roughly 200, plus modest program income, generates maybe $160,000 to $240,000 in a good year. The gap is $60,000 to $140,000 annually. That is the real number. It is not catastrophic — it is, in fact, modest for a facility of this age and significance — but it is a loss, and the Y is using that loss as justification for introducing pickleball, displacing tennis hours, dismissing the tennis director, and slowly strangling a community that has sustained itself for half a century.

The institution that cannot generate a surplus on a gifted $48 million facility is now dismantling a $2 million facility that was self-sustaining until the institution's own management degraded it. The palace is subsidizing its own inefficiency by cannibalizing the cottage. And the plan for the cottage is the same as the plan for everything else.

*

The palace on 24th Avenue is real and it is beautiful and no doubt many people use it and benefit from it.

The question I keep returning to, as a bemused observer of the modern bureaucratic state, is a simple one:

If this organization cannot generate a surplus on a gifted $48 million facility, exempt from all taxes, and adds another $3 million to a mortgage, in a market where it voluntarily prices below its own rack rate — what, exactly, is the plan?

The answer, I suspect, is the same as it always has been.

Another campaign.

Chapter 9: The Smoke Machine

Gaslightery Indeed

"Transparency is like sincerity. It works like a charm once you manage to fake it."

On February 25th, we attended the meeting.

We learned what transparency means in this particular context.

It means: we will tell you what we have already decided, in a format that discourages questions, on a timeline of our choosing, without an agenda, and we will call the whole thing a listening session. You are welcome to feel heard. Feeling heard and being heard are, in the modern institutional vocabulary, the same thing.

For sixty minutes, Brian, Cindie, and Beth presented their vision. The word "transparent" appeared several times. The agenda did not appear at all, because there was no agenda — a fact that, on reflection, tells you everything you need to know about what kind of listening was planned.

A note on the presenters. Three people who have never learned to play tennis were confidently redesigning a tennis center with all sorts of new things. Shiny things, in the parlance. More pickleball times to "serve" the pickleball community. Great group lessons for tennis and pickleball to really get this thing off the ground. Brian's most proximate connection to the sport: his daughter plays on a high school team, so he is a fan. This is like having a kid who likes chemistry take apart your 4Runner to look for an oil leak.

Since the meeting, I have been curating a small museum of transparency. Consider it a guided tour.

Exhibit A: The Dispositive Metrics

The February 25th presentation rested heavily on usage metrics — data points drawn from USTA measurement frameworks demonstrating, conclusively, that the Tennis Center was underutilized. The metrics were presented as dispositive. Case closed. The numbers don't lie.

There is, however, a detail worth mentioning.

The United States Tennis Association, whose metrics were cited as the authoritative basis for this analysis, has itself advised against using those particular measurements for tennis center evaluation. The methodology is outdated, the USTA has said, and should not be applied to determine the health or viability of a tennis facility.

So the weapon of choice — the objective, data-driven, scientific evidence that tennis is failing — was drawn from a source that has specifically recommended against using it for this purpose.

This is not a transparency problem exactly. It is something adjacent: the confident deployment of authoritative-sounding evidence that, on inspection, does not say what it is presented as saying. In a court of law it would be called misleading. In a PowerPoint presentation to the Oh Gosh Brigade, it is called "messaging."

In the vernacular we call it blowing smoke.

Exhibit B: The Selfish Tennis Community

One corporate communication made a striking argument: that the Tennis Center, by occupying so much square footage and so many court hours, was essentially being subsidized by the general YMCA membership. Tennis members, the implication ran, were taking more than their share.

This argument has a certain logic, if you decide that the Tennis Center sprang spontaneously to life a few months ago and omit everything that came before.

If you begin the history in the late 1970s, however, when it actually began, the argument becomes somewhat harder to sustain. The Tennis Center was not built with YMCA funds. It was not built on the YMCA's initiative. It was conceived, funded, and constructed by the Eugene tennis community on YMCA land, pursuant to a mutual understanding: we build it, you operate it as a tennis center, we support it indefinitely. For forty-five years, the tennis community paid a premium membership — $924 per year against the general membership's effective average of roughly $200 — and that steady premium revenue, particularly during the financially difficult years of the early 1990s, helped keep the main YMCA solvent.

The Tennis Center has been subsidizing the YMCA. The YMCA has not been subsidizing the Tennis Center.

Describing this relationship as tennis hogging square footage at the expense of other members is, in the technical sense, the opposite of what happened. It is also, in the Orwellian sense, a rewriting of history sufficiently confident that it expects not to be checked. There is a clinical term for telling people that their lived experience is the opposite of what it actually was. The term is gaslighting.

Exhibit C: The Private Lesson Racket

Here is a transparency puzzle worth puzzling over.

The official justification for reducing tennis court hours and expanding pickleball access is usage. Tennis courts with only two (singles) or four (doubles) players on for a slot leaves so much empty space. But pickleball solves that space metric by putting as many as sixteen joyful pickleballers onto a single court, smashing wiffleballs and shouting to be heard and screaming with delight.

At the same time, a significant portion of court time has been quietly reserved for private tennis lessons at a surcharge of $70 per session — lessons available primarily to members who can afford the premium, and whose lesson time is effectively protected from the pickleball incursion that has displaced regular tennis members. Not counting the tennis coach, the metric is now one person per court per slot. Several have told me that they don't really want to take a lesson but, given the scarcity of court time, it's one way they can guarantee a certain amount of tennis per week.

So: regular tennis players are told their court hours must be reduced because usage is low and the space must be shared. Meanwhile, a premium-priced private lesson economy quietly operates on the same courts, generating revenue, and apparently exempt from the sharing imperative.

The transparency question is not complicated: which goal is actually driving the decision? Utilization? Community access? Or the $70 surcharge?

Exhibit D: The $11 Million Estimate

At some point in recent months, the YMCA floated a figure in a transparency messaging email: adding two tennis courts and adjusting the parking lot would cost $11 million. This number was offered as a reason why expansion was not feasible. Case closed.

I mentioned this figure to several builder friends. The laughter lasted a while. Each of them offered to build not two but four new courts plus parking for $5 million. My own estimate, with full YMCA cooperation, would be closer to $3 million.

If the $11 million number was accurate, the existing four-court facility by itself, as is, where is — built on the same structural logic — would be worth $22 million. This would make the original tennis community's fundraising achievement quite spectacular. I do not believe the YMCA intends to value it at $22 million.

The $11 million figure has one of two explanations. Either it reflects a genuine cost analysis conducted by a

clueless someone who has not recently priced a Butler
Building, or it was offered with the ulterior motive that a
large number would end the conversation.

Some of us, it turns out, have built things before.

*

After the meeting, a guy approached me in the lobby.
He wanted to defend the institution's feelings. Not its
mission, not its record, not its promises — its feelings.
The staff works so hard, he said. The people who built the
new facility care deeply. My observation that the new
building had lost most of the soul of the old decrepit
place was, in his view, an insult to the people who had
given so much. Feelings, so many feelings.

I told him, very nicely, that I didn't care what he felt,
and that I meant it. This is not a conversation about
feelings. This is a conversation about ethics, promises,
money, and stewardship of a tennis center that requires
the original and continuing promises to be kept.

*

A word about Orwell, since he is already in the room.

In "Politics and the English Language" he wrote that
political language — and by extension institutional
language — is designed to make lies sound truthful and
murder respectable, and to give an appearance of solidity
to pure wind. The dialect has a few signature moves.
Passive constructions that eliminate actors: decisions
were made, changes were implemented, concerns were
noted. Abstract nouns that replace specific claims: vision,
community, outcomes, impact. And above all, the
deployment of process language — listening sessions,
consultant engagements, strategic planning frameworks
— that creates the impression of deliberation while
foreclosing the possibility of any result other than the
one already decided.

The tennis community has been subjected to this
dialect for two years now. We have received its

communications, attended its messaging sessions, and waited for its processes to conclude. We have been told, repeatedly, that our concerns have been heard.

Heard is not the same as answered. Listening is not the same as responding. Transparency is not the same as honesty.

*

Let me offer a working definition, assembled from the evidence.

Transparency, at the Eugene Family YMCA, means: we will use metrics that the issuing authority has warned against using. We will describe a forty-five year subsidy relationship as its opposite. We will protect premium-revenue court time while citing utilization concerns to displace regular members. We will offer cost estimates that cause professional builders to laugh. We will schedule a listening session without an agenda, present for sixty minutes, take whatever "incoming" there is and declare the result a community conversation. We will redescribe your experience until you doubt your own memory, and we will call that messaging.

And we will use the word transparent throughout, because the word does useful work. It suggests openness while practicing its opposite. It implies that the institution has nothing to hide, which discourages looking.

*

One last thing.

On the evening of February 25th, while the YMCA leadership team was inside the Glass Palace explaining their vision with a sixty-minute PowerPoint, a taco truck was parked outside doing brisk business.

No consultant required. No 990 showing $220K in losses. No $3 million in new liabilities. No sixty-minute PowerPoint. No listening session without an agenda. The taco truck knows exactly who its customer is. It shows up

when the customer is there. It sells one thing and sells it
well. It turns a profit because it has to — there is no
501(c)(3) umbrella to fund the truck purchase, absorb
the losses, no donor campaign to paper over the
operating gap, no lottery bonds to build the kitchen.

The $48 million Glass Palace lost $220,000 last year
serving its community. Manuel's taco truck parked
outside hit its numbers, is grinding out an annual ROI of
30% and will pay the vehicle loan and food prep costs in
a superbly timely manner. Manuel has never even
thought of hiring a consultant.

Manuel doesn't need a listening session. He already
knows what you want. It's on the menu.

Chapter 10: What You Bring
On Offering Something Instead of Nothing

"If you can bring nothing to this place but your carcass, keep out." — William Carlos Williams, "Dedication for a Plot of Ground"

Williams wrote that line about his grandmother — an immigrant who had fought for everything she ever had. It was not an insult. It was a standard. If you are going to stand on this ground, you had better bring something more than the fact of your presence. You had better bring work, or love, or a plan, or at the very least the willingness to build something that wasn't here before you arrived.

I have been thinking about that line for years, since I was a first year English major in 1972, when I had every Williams volume published by the New Directions publishing house. The sentence applies — with uncomfortable precision — to the modern habit of showing up to every argument, every institution, every broken situation with nothing but opinion. Nothing but complaint. Nothing but your collected carcass of whinging.

There is no shortage of people who can tell you what's wrong. Pick any subject and you will find an unlimited supply of intelligent people describing the problem with great precision, great feeling, and absolutely no intention of doing anything about it.

If all I had to offer was that stuff, I would have stopped before typing Word One.

I want to say that plainly, at the top, because this series has been critical — deliberately, necessarily, and at length. I already spent thousands of words on the history of the Tennis Center, its magical elements, the decisions that are damaging it, the community survey that was designed not to discover the truth but to manufacture it in a preferred form, and the institutional posture that treated forty-seven years of community stewardship as an inconvenience to be assumed away. I meant every word, and I stand behind all of it.

But I am not going through all of this to just end up with a negative, to be the most verbose squawker on the subject. That is not who I am. If I didn't see a very positive outcome — a beautiful one, actually — I would fold my tent, get on my camel, and caravan to the next oasis.

I have a plan. And I think it is a thing of beauty, but then again I am a positivist and an enthusiast at heart. Now, before I lay the plan out in detail — that is the next essay — I want to talk about something I haven't introduced in this series, something that has been running underneath it from the beginning, because it's not only the way I roll, it's the only way I roll.

————

The Moral Philosophy You're Already Living

Go ahead and yawn but it's high time to talk about moral philosophy. Not the kind you study in a university — Aristotle, Kant, Hume, Nietzsche, men who spent their lives in ivory towers of the mind arguing about right and wrong. You could fill a wall with their books. That's where the egghead version of moral philosophy lived and still lives, but it's not where actual moral philosophy lives.

Moral philosophy lives in ordinary people who, on ordinary days, must make ordinary decisions. Every one of us is a moral philosopher by necessity — not by choice. The moment you wake up and begin interacting with the world, you are deciding what matters, how to behave, what is right, what is tolerable, and what is not.

Over the years — on a ranch, mostly, where bad decisions break things immediately and visibly — I now think there are really only two directions a person can go. You can live with a kind of faith in goodness, or you can drift into a kind of faith in something else. We will find out that it is, in fact, evil. Not dramatic evil. Not the kind you read about in history books. Just the quiet, everyday version. The small corrosive permissions. The little compromises. The moment you say, this doesn't matter. The moment you look away.

I believe the good direction is Grace.

In the book I am writing — *Grace: The Navigator's Guide* — I describe four rules of Grace: surrender, attention, gratitude, and generosity. That is the operating system — the way a life works when it is running well. But an operating system needs applications, and what I want to show here is what those rules look like when they leave the page and enter a room where something real is at stake.

First, surrender. Let go of the idea that if you do enough things correctly you will be able to control everything. Forget that magical thinking. Accept that you are not in charge of the whole world — or even a small part of it.

Second, pay attention. Actually see what is happening. See people clearly. See situations clearly. Most trouble comes from not really looking.

Third, take the next right action. Not the perfect action. Not the clever action. Just the honest one which is required of you, now. It will always be the fair one, and the one you know, quietly, is right.

Fourth, accept and be grateful. Take the result as it comes. Don't twist yourself into resentment. Don't keep score.

And then there is the opposite approach which will guide you into evil's grasp. Refuse to surrender — insist on control. Distort reality — see what you want to see, and require others to see it as well. Make rules and

judgments for everyone, and grow exasperated when
they don't care. Act for yourself alone — take the short
gain, use people if necessary, protect your position. Live
in resentment — blame others, stay aggrieved, and
assume the world is against you.

————

Two Women Who Saw This Clearly

I arrived at this framework independently after way
too much trial and error, but I am not the first person to
see it.

Simone Weil, writing in France in the early 1940s
while the world was literally falling apart around her,
built her entire moral philosophy on the concept of
attention — not concentration, not focus, but a radical
openness to reality that requires setting aside the ego.
She wrote that attention means encountering people and
situations as they truly are, not as your ego needs them
to be. "Attention is the rarest and purest form of
generosity," she wrote.

But Weil went further. In her book *Gravity and Grace*,
she argued that there are two forces operating on the
human soul. Gravity is the natural downward pull — ego,
self-interest, the mechanical self-protection that makes
people smaller and meaner by degrees. Grace is what
can interrupt that pull.

"All the natural movements of the soul are controlled
by laws similar to gravity," Weil wrote, "except grace."

She died at thirty-four. Albert Camus called her the
only great spirit of her time.

Iris Murdoch picked up where Weil left off. Writing in
England in the 1960s and 70s, Murdoch argued in *The
Sovereignty of Good* that the central obstacle to the
moral life is what she memorably called "the fat
relentless ego." Her solution was what she called

unselfing: turning attention outward, away from your own grievances, toward reality as it actually is.

Murdoch illustrated it with a scene, remarkable in its simplicity. You are looking out a window, brooding over some damage done to your prestige, and suddenly you notice a kestrel hovering outside. In that moment, the ego drops away. You see something real instead of your own grievance. Everything shifts.

That shift — from brooding to seeing — is the hinge of the whole thing. It is the difference between the two paths. And it is available at any moment, in any conflict, to anyone willing to look up.

————

What the Critical Essays Were Actually Doing

Now. Why am I telling you this in a series about a tennis center?

Because I realized, looking back at the tennis war essays, that these steps are exactly what happened — not as a program I followed consciously, but as a pattern.

The critical essays — the history, the documentation, the survey analysis, the institutional critique — that was step two. *Pay attention.* You can't build something real on top of a distorted picture.

The paying-attention phase looks like negativity to people who would rather not look. It is not. It is the foundation. I spent 3,500 words dismantling the survey, and I make no apology for a single word of it.

But there comes a point where the critical work is done — or done enough — and staying in it will mean crossing over to the other path. Murdoch's ever-narrowing cycles.

It is time to shift gears.

————

So I Built Something

William James wrote something that informs this experience for me. "Be not afraid of life. Believe that life is worth living, and your belief will help create the fact."

He was not being mystical. He was being practical. James argued that faith in an outcome is often a necessary condition for that outcome.

So I sat down — by myself, over a period of weeks — and designed a solution where everyone would win. Kurt Hahn basically said that the problem you have is your opportunity, the obstacle you confront isn't the obstacle at all, but rather it is the path.

I didn't design a petition, a manifesto, or a counter-argument. I worked through 10 or 12 iterations and produced a working plan, with a governance structure, a financial model, a phased construction timeline, a revenue projection, and a thirty-year outlook.

The Eugene Y Tennis Academy: an independent nonprofit that partners with the YMCA to operate a world-class tennis facility on the existing site.

It is an exciting idea. It was when I first wrote it and it still is when I look at it. It's an idea that is a dream, and it can be all of ours.

The tennis community builds it. The tennis community funds it. The tennis community governs it. The Y receives a revenue stream — conservatively $315,000 per year, optimistically $585,000 — with zero operational burden. Over thirty years, that is between $9 million and $17 million flowing to the Y. The Y keeps the land. The Y keeps the facility. The Y keeps the fame and the glory. And the Y does not spend a dollar to make it happen.

That is the plan in compressed form. The next essay lays it all out.

————

What I Did With It

Here is a part that matters for this essay — the part that connects the plan back to the philosophy.

I did not publish it or talk about it until now. I did not wave it around. I put it together and sent it quietly to the person who runs the YMCA, so that he could see the path and, if he chose, take the credit for walking it. I offered it with a single line that I think captures the whole approach:

The credit for all of it belongs to the Board that said yes.

That line is step three and step four, rolled into one sentence. Take the next right action — which in this case meant building something useful and handing it to the person who needed it. And then accept what comes — which means letting go of credit, letting go of the outcome, letting the institution take the glory if they have the courage to say yes.

I don't need the credit. I need the tennis center to continue and flourish beyond my lifetime.

James also wrote: "The great use of life is to spend it for something that will outlast it." That is what I am trying to do.

————

The Other Path

I should say a word about what the Y has proposed instead, while dismissing the elegant tennis academy plan, because the contrast is instructive.

Their concept is to continue to minimize the tennis part of the Tennis Center by using it as a sort of grab-bag for whatever use appeals to someone with leverage and an office in the glass palace on 24th Avenue, and to build multipurpose structures on the remainder of that unique, magical site. The estimated cost is $12 million, which would need to be raised in a metro area where the combined city populations of Eugene and Springfield total about 240,000.

But the money is not even the real problem. The real problem is that the Y's jumble plan is a boring idea. There is nothing distinctive about it. There is nothing in it that earns a meeting with Nike or a call from the USTA or a feature in any publication. It has no soul.

And underneath all of it is a question of scale that nobody at the Y seems to be asking. The Eugene Family YMCA currently operates a major facility serving roughly 25,000 members. If the expansion plans proceed — two additional Y facilities in Eugene/Springfield — you are looking at a nonprofit that aspires to serve roughly 75,000 members in a combined urban population of about 240,000 people. That is over 30 percent of the entire community, served by a single nonprofit institution. At some point, that stops being community service and starts being something else — an empire of good intentions, perhaps, but an empire nonetheless.

————

The Offering

So here we are.

On their side, a $12 million plan to build something ordinary and destroy something irreplaceable in the process. On our side, a roughly $2.3 million plan — community-funded, community-built, community-governed — to build something extraordinary and preserve what already exists.

One path requires the institution to raise money it does not have, for a vision it cannot articulate, in a market that has no reason to care. The other asks the institution to do one thing: say yes. And then let the people who built this place forty-seven years ago finish what they started.

William Carlos Williams understood this. He spent his entire life as a doctor in Rutherford, New Jersey, delivering babies and treating the sick, and then writing some of the most original American poetry ever at his kitchen table after the house calls were done. He did not wait for ideal conditions. He brought what he had. "No ideas but in things," he wrote — meaning: stop talking about abstractions and put something real on the table.

That is what I have tried to do.

In the next essay, I will lay the whole plan out in detail — the Academy, the finances, the geography, the partnerships, the vision. I am going to make the case as clearly as I can, and then I am going to leave it there for the entire community to pick it up and evaluate the dream.

Because in the end, what you bring to the world is the one thing that is entirely, inescapably, yours. Not the result. Not the credit. Not the outcome.

The offering.

Chapter 11: The Eugene Y Tennis Academy

The Plan, the Numbers, and a Gift for Whoever Wants It

Tennis Town U.S.A.???

In the previous essay I said I had a plan, and that I thought it was a thing of beauty. Here it is.

What follows is the full proposal for the Eugene Y Tennis Academy — an independent nonprofit that would partner with the Eugene Family YMCA to operate a world-class tennis facility at the existing Tennis Center site. Everything is here: the vision, the governance, the construction, the financials, the thirty-year outlook, and the three paths the Y can choose among.

I am making this public because the community that built the Tennis Center forty-seven years ago deserves to see what is possible — and because the best ideas get better when more people can see them, challenge them, and improve them.

This is a first concept. It would give way to multiple iterations as better minds and more experienced hands shape it. But the direction is right, the numbers work, and the idea has something that no amount of institutional planning can manufacture: a soul.

———

The Geography Nobody Is Discussing

The Eugene Family YMCA Tennis Center sits at the center of one of the most remarkable athletic corridors in the American West. Within a one-mile radius:

South Eugene High School — one of Oregon's premier varsity tennis programs — directly across the street.

University of Oregon Tennis — now a Big Ten program — less than half a mile away.

Hayward Field — the most storied track and field venue in America, the heart of Track Town USA.

No other YMCA in America sits at this intersection. That is not a marketing claim — it is a fact of geography. And geography, properly leveraged, is destiny.

The Tennis Center is not an isolated facility with a cost problem. It is the geographical anchor of a potential athletic partnership triangle that no national brand, no USTA regional director, and no sports media outlet has yet been asked to consider.

————

The Model Already Exists — One Mile Away

Before describing the Academy in detail, I want to draw your attention to something hiding in plain sight.

One mile from the Tennis Center sits Hayward Field — arguably the most celebrated track and field venue in America. What the University of Oregon and the Eugene community built there did not happen by accident. It happened because a group of people had the vision to layer events: state high school championships, regional high school meets, college invitationals, NCAA Championships, and ultimately world-class professional and international competitions. Track Town USA is not a tagline. It is an identity built one event at a time, over decades, through exactly the kind of institutional partnership and community commitment we are proposing for tennis.

The University of Oregon has a superb 6-court indoor tennis facility with stands and multiple outdoor courts — facilities which are empty probably 80% of the time, and even more during the summer tournament season. That facility, combined with 8 indoor courts at the Tennis Center and 4 outdoor courts at South Eugene High

School, plus the courts available across town at the Eugene Swim and Tennis Club, creates something no single institution in this corridor currently possesses: a regional tennis infrastructure capable of hosting events at every level.

The Track Town USA model is not a metaphor. It is a blueprint.

Think about it: *Tennis Town USA*. It has a nice, if a bit familiar, ring to it.

————

The Proposed Institution

The Eugene Y Tennis Academy would be established as an independent 501(c)(3) nonprofit organization — governed by an Autonomous Governing Board (AGB) that includes: a YMCA representative as a full voting board member, Tennis Center community members, South Eugene High School tennis representation, independent directors, and open seats for University of Oregon and other institutional partners who choose to participate.

This structure protects both parties. The Academy gains the governance stability it needs to execute a long-range vision. The Y gains a well-run, revenue-generating partner that enhances its facility and reputation — without the operational burden of running a world-class tennis program.

Two governance connections matter:

First, the AGB will include a YMCA representative as a full voting board member — ensuring the Y has real standing and real authority in the Academy's direction.

Second, the YMCA Board itself should include a member who represents the Tennis Center and the tennis community — ensuring that the Academy's perspective is heard at the institutional level.

This dual connection is what makes the partnership durable. The Academy is not a tenant. It is a partner.

The Physical Plan — Phased Construction

The construction plan is deliberately realistic. Community-build methodology — the same approach used to construct the original 1970s facility — cuts approximately $1,000,000 off total costs before the first nail is driven.

Phase 1 (Year 1): Restore existing 4 courts and facilities. Estimated cost: $320,000–$400,000. Community-build discount: $80,000–$100,000.

Phase 2 (Years 2–3): Add 4 new indoor courts, expanding to 8 total. Estimated cost: $2,000,000–$3,000,000. Community-build discount: $500,000–$750,000.

Total estimated cost range: $2,320,000–$3,400,000.

For reference: a consultant estimate presented at the February 25 Y board meeting priced 2 indoor courts at $12,000,000. The community estimates above price 4 courts at $2.32M–$3.4M.

————

The Program Suite

The Academy operates on a revenue-sharing model for tennis professionals — not salary overhead. This keeps fixed costs low, aligns instructor incentives with program quality, and scales naturally with enrollment.

Programs include: Junior Academy (ages 5–18) with tiered development, Adult Programs (clinics, leagues, drop-in), Tournament Hosting (USTA sanctioned events), Private Instruction (revenue-share model), Community Access (open court time for members), and Summer Camps.

A note on member court access: the Academy will offer robust reservation slots for members, with a wise and seasonally adjusting allocation across available resources. In the summer months, outdoor courts at South Eugene High School will be available for reservations as well.

————

The National Sponsorship Opportunity

This is the dimension of the proposal that a local YMCA cannot access on its own — and it is the dimension that transforms the Academy from a local tennis program into a nationally significant institution.

Nike, Wilson, Head, and the USTA all have sponsored tennis programs. None of them sponsors a neighborhood YMCA tennis center. The reason is simple: the story is too small.

The Eugene Y Tennis Academy is a categorically different proposition. Consider the sponsorship pitch: The only YMCA tennis facility in America in a Big Ten athletic corridor. A junior-to-collegiate pipeline: YMCA Academy to South Eugene High School to University of Oregon. 8 indoor plus 4 outdoor courts — a credible regional tournament host. Located in Track Town USA — one of the most media-saturated athletic environments in America. A nearly 50-year community story — authenticity no constructed facility can replicate.

That pitch earns a meeting with Nike's community sports division. It earns a call from Wilson's partnership team.

"The Tennis Y Out West" — a brand identity that no other YMCA in America possesses.

————

The Financial Model

Current State

The Y does not publish Tennis Center-specific financials. The estimates below are based on observable staffing levels, current membership pricing, and the Y's own 990 filings. They are conservative.

Current estimated revenue: $160,000–$240,000. Current estimated expenses: $302,000. Current estimated annual loss: $62,000–$142,000.

Academy Revenue Model — Year 3 Steady State

Conservative scenario (500 members): Total revenue $665,000. Optimistic scenario (800 members): Total revenue $935,000.

Conservative operating expenses: $350,000. Optimistic operating expenses: $350,000.

Conservative annual surplus: $315,000. Optimistic annual surplus: $585,000.

Y Facility Fee (paid by Academy to Y): $450 per member per year.

30-Year Y Revenue — Facility Fees Only

Conservative (500 members): $9,450,000 cumulative. Optimistic (800 members): $17,550,000 cumulative.

For context: the entire parcel, if sold today, is estimated at approximately $3,000,000. The Academy's conservative 30-year facility fee projection alone exceeds that by $6.45M — while the Y retains the land, the facility, and the institutional distinction.

————

Three Paths Forward

Path 1 — Status Quo: The Cost of Drift

Doing nothing is not a neutral choice. Estimated $100,000–$150,000 in net operating losses per year — compounding. Active tennis membership has declined from a historic 500 to approximately 200. Status quo is not a holding pattern. It is a slow-motion version of the worst-case outcome.

Path 2 — Sale of the Parcel

The parcel is estimated at approximately $3,000,000.
The Y's 2024 total liabilities are approximately $9.4
million — roughly three times the parcel value. Sale of a
community-funded charitable asset raises serious
questions under Oregon nonprofit law. The reputational
cost is permanent.

Path 3 — The Academy: The One Path with Genuine Upside

The Academy is the only path that solves all four of
the Y's problems simultaneously: It eliminates the
operating loss and replaces it with guaranteed revenue.
It removes the management burden from Y staff. It
requires zero capital from the Y. It creates a national
institutional identity.

The Y does not need to build this. It does not need to
fund this. It does not need to manage this. It needs to say
yes — and then let the community that has been trying to
give it a gift for 47 years finish the job.

————

A Necessary First Step

I want to be direct about one thing that I regard as
an essential first step for any path forward to succeed:
the tennis courts must be returned to tennis — fully and
exclusively.

This is not a tactical point. It is a foundational one.
The restoration of the courts to tennis is the single most
visible signal the Y can send that the relationship is being
repaired — and it costs nothing.

————

What We Are Asking For

Three things:

First, a genuine commitment to tennis as the sole and
primary use of the tennis courts.

Second, the establishment of an Autonomous Governing Board — with a YMCA representative as a full voting member, and a parallel commitment to seat a Tennis Center representative on the YMCA Board itself.

Third, a formal commitment to begin work with the AGB on the Eugene Y Tennis Academy plan — with the understanding that the tennis community is prepared to help build, fund, and govern what it is proposing.

———

The People Are Ready

This is not a proposal in search of leadership. We have capable, respected, and successful people in this community who are already well suited to doing exactly what this moment requires.

I didn't create this plan to score points. I fashioned it because I saw a clear path that works for everyone — the Y, the tennis players, the high school, the university, and the city. The numbers are real. The geography is real. The people are real.

All that is needed now is a handshake.

We have accepted those before.

The credit for all of it belongs to the Board that said yes.

Chapter 12: The Summer of '42

The Final Chapter?

The cathedral of tennis . . .

I

It is a Saturday morning, late June, 2042. A spectacular day.

Justin Jacobsen is eighteen and has driven seventeen hundred miles from Omaha to Eugene, to attend the University of Oregon, in large part because he had "big tennis dreams" as a kid, took lessons, went to a Nike camp, played first singles on his high school team and went to the Nebraska state championships and lost, badly, two years in a row. Still he has tennis posters on his wall and the family is a tennis family. He had dreamed of attending the Tennis Academy in Eugene, but it had never quite worked out.

Justin is not a tournament-level player. Not a Division One recruit. But he has always wanted to go to school as a Duck, and connect to this place that is becoming a central nerve in American tennis, which is in a strong revival.

The academy is now fifteen years old and bigger than anyone had dreamed. There are three separate campuses: the original Patterson Avenue facility which now has eight indoor courts and eight outdoor courts, a five court facility with two outdoor clay courts in West Eugene near the Walmart, and a new twenty-court complex in Beaverton where three of the top junior players in the world—junior slam winners, all American-born—are training alongside four top juniors from overseas.

Justin locks his old-school bike to the rack on Patterson and walks in. He is like those running enthusiasts visiting the spot where Steve Prefontaine died in his sports car. This is a pilgrimage.

The first thing that surprises him is the old-timers.

On Court Three, two men are playing singles. They have the stiff spines of guys whose lowest vertebrae fused more than forty years ago, and bird legs, and the flattened asses of age, and Justin wonders—his dad is an orthopedist—how many of their joints are replacement equipment. Probably at least one hip and two knees between them is his guess.

They finish their match and exit the courts faster than you'd expect. They still have some zip in them, these fossils.

The girl at the desk, Amber Lee, is a freshman at the University of Oregon, on the tennis team, and a graduate of this academy. She has just finished taking the "old juniors"—twelve-year-olds—through their practice sessions. Justin recognizes her from the party the night before; he had mentioned his tennis background, but now it might seem just a little too proudly.

"Hi there, again."

"Oh yeah. Hi again."

"You work here?"

"For over five years."

"Did you go here? Is this where you—"

She nods and smiles and then turns her attention to the old guys.

"How was the match, gentlemen?"

"We both stayed upright, so there's that. Had some great points."

"Who won?"

"David always beats me."

"Not always."

Amber Lee turns back to Justin. "Did you want to join the Academy as a playing member?"

"I can do that? I didn't know I could."

"Sure, you can join and then we can play without you having to get a guest pass. Ever since the first expansion in 2027 it's always been a double threat: tennis academy and tennis center for the townies." She pauses. "You'll probably want to become a member . . . for the beatings I will administer."

Justin laughs. He fills out the form on the tablet at the desk while the two old guys sit down in the lounge area with water bottles and start a conversation about something. Justin tries to catch it, he is curious enough about these geezers that he eavesdrops.

". . . so, the field rotates even if the tracking is perfect?"

"On an alt-az mount, yes. But, ah, you need a de-rotator or you get star trails at the edge of the frame. It's a trig problem but . . ."

Justin smiles to himself: he hears every single word and it means zero to him.

The place is not what he expected. He'd seen the photos online—the old building, the original four courts from the seventies, the building addition that doubled the size. But photos didn't capture the sheer energy. There are kids everywhere. Not little kids, not beginners—real players, twelve- and thirteen-year-olds hitting with an intensity that makes him reassess whether he actually wants Amber Lee to see his forehand.

"Who are all these kids?"

"Saturday morning academy session. The twelves and the fourteens. The older kids train in Beaverton now, at the new facility, but the younger ones all come through here first. This is where it starts."

"And those two?" He nods toward the old guys, who have moved on from astrophotography to a new restaurant in town and some sadness that Bill, recently passed, will never eat there. Old man talk.

"They've been playing here since before I was born. Since before my mom was born, I think. They're here every Tuesday and Thursday. I'm not sure why they're here today on a Saturday, but I'd guess it's because one of them can't make next Tuesday."

"How old are they?"

"Shh, not so loud, that's not polite." She pauses. "Eighties. Late eighties maybe."

Justin looks around the lobby. There are photos on the wall near the entrance. A timeline. Black-and-white shots of guys in short shorts with wooden rackets standing in front of what looks like a barn. A construction photo with a half-finished steel frame. A group portrait— maybe forty people, some couples, a few guys in suits, some in tennis whites—with a caption he can't read from the desk.

"What's that picture? The big group one."

"The original founders. Nineteen seventy-seven. They built the first courts with a handshake and their own money. There's a plaque outside but nobody reads it."

"I read it," one of the old guys calls out. "I read it every time I come in."

"That's because you knew them, Tom."

"I knew some of them. The ones who were still around when I started. I met and talked with all the widows about this place back when it was on life support in the mid twenties."

Justin finishes the form and gives it to Amber. She hands him a membership badge. It has the academy logo on it—a simple line drawing of a court viewed through a cathedral window, which he thinks is cool but doesn't entirely understand.

"Court six is open," she says. "I'm off in five minutes. Get warmed up. You'll need it."

He walks through the double doors onto the court level and stops. Eight courts on this side, all occupied or reserved. Through the glass partition he can see the newer building—four more courts, higher ceilings, better lighting. A coach is feeding balls to a girl who can't be older than eight but moves like she's been doing this since she could walk.

He finds court six and starts hitting against the wall.

Through the window he can see the parking lot, and beyond it Patterson Avenue, and beyond that the high school courts. It is a late June morning and everything is green in the way that only Oregon is green, and he is inside a building that he'd traveled seventeen hundred miles to visit because he'd read about it and wanted to see if it was real.

It is real.

Amber Lee appears on the other side of the net with two cans of balls and a racket bag stuffed with tennis things. She pulls out a racquet, one of about six in there, and it looks like it has seen serious work.

"Ready?"

"No."

"Good. That's the right answer."

————

II

It's the same Saturday morning, late June, 2042. A spectacular day.

Justin Jacobsen is eighteen, a freshman at the University of Oregon, and he is looking for a tennis court. He'd met a girl at a party the night before and she said she could beat him and he said prove it and she said tomorrow, ten o'clock, the city courts on Patterson, near 21st. Not that many people his age played tennis anymore. The magnificent sport was now dominated completely by Europe, the long forty year descent that began, interestingly enough, when Roger Federer bounced Pete Sampras off Wimbledon in 2001 in five sets.

It was 10:03 on his phone.

He rode his old-school bike to the corner of Patterson and 20th and, looking west, saw a high school where he thought he should see tennis courts. The girl, Amber Lee, had said "20th and Patterson." At least he thought so. To his left, running the full two blocks from 20th to 22nd and filling the entire stretch of Patterson to Hilyard, stood a three-story medical complex. Tinted glass and beige siding. Dentists, podiatrists, an urgent care facility. It seemed a little out of place.

An old guy was standing in front of it, not going in, not leaving, just standing there staring at the building and then glancing across the street at the high school's playing fields.

To an eighteen-year-old, anyone over thirty seems old. But this old timer was ancient. He could croak on the spot, Justin thought to himself. And he was just standing there, looking at the building as if he thought it might vanish any second.

"Sir. Do you know where the tennis courts are?"

"What? Sorry. I was lost in something there for a while."

"I'm supposed to play tennis with a girl here. She said 20th and Patterson."

"She said 20th and Patterson, did she? Amazing."

"Yeah, I think that's what she said. We didn't exchange numbers, I guess she thought this would be an old school test of my interest."

"The courts at 20th and Patterson. Well, you're about twenty years too late, Sonny. Sorry."

This old guy seemed a little addled.

"Say what?"

"They finally tore that tennis center down in 2030, 2031. When the doctors put together the money for the place that—well, became this place. Took out the entire line of little houses on the Hilyard side; nobody misses those, I suppose."

Seeing him up closer, the old guy was really old. Maybe ten years older than Justin's grandfather, who was on dialysis. Still, he looked okay. He was wearing new kicks, K-Swiss tennis kicks. You didn't see those every day. And now that he was remembering stuff from the old days, he seemed to be on top of things. Or maybe he was just making it up.

"The last time I played here was in September, 2028. They kept the original four courts going right up to the end but it was just reservation tennis by then, and nobody cared about the place. I played a Wednesday singles game with David. We knew it was the last time."

"So what happened?"

"That's a long story, could fill a book, to be honest. Short version is, the people who ran it didn't want to run it anymore. Whether by design or negligence every step they took subtracted more and more of whatever was left. The people who wanted to save it couldn't get anyone to listen."

"Well, that sucks."

"Yeah. It does."

Justin looked at the medical building. There was a Subway on the ground floor, which struck him as depressing but he couldn't have said why.

"Were the courts any good?"

The old man laughed. It was a real laugh, not a sad one, which surprised Justin.

"Four indoor courts. The only dedicated indoor tennis facility built by a YMCA in the entire northwest, maybe the whole country, who knows anymore? In this climate, covered courts were gold. We had guys in their eighties who played three times a week. A guy named David and I played every Wednesday for twenty-seven years. Every Wednesday."

"Twenty-seven years?"

"Every Wednesday."

Justin didn't know what to say to that. He checked his phone. 10:11.

"So, there's nowhere to play around here? What was that girl trying to pull?"

The old man came back from wherever he'd been.

"Oh—you want the city courts. That's where she is. They're on 24th. Go south two blocks, take a right. There's a big apartment complex, can't miss it. The courts are just inside, kind of tucked behind the parking garage. Not really on Patterson, but I guess that's the closest cross street."

"Thanks."

"She any good? This girl?"

"She says she is."

"Then you'd better get moving. You're already late."

Justin pedaled off. The old man watched him go, then looked back at the building for another minute. Then he walked to his car, which was parked on 20th, and drove home. No more tennis for him, but it was a clear night tonight and he always had permission from the rancher to set up his cameras and see what turned up.

————

III

One of these Saturday mornings is going to happen.

Not metaphorically. Not as a thought experiment. One of these mornings—a real morning, with real sun on Patterson Avenue and a real kid on a real bike—is sixteen years from now. The kid exists already. He's two years old. He's toddling around somewhere, right now, maybe in Omaha, Nebraska, you can never tell. Anyway he has no idea that a building in Eugene, Oregon, is going to matter to him a lot.

Or not.

The courts exist already. Four of them, under a roof that thirty-six people paid for with their own money in 1977 because nobody else was going to do it. Those courts are still there this morning. They were there yesterday. They will be there tomorrow.

The question is whether they will be there in 2042.

That is not a question about money. The money exists. It is not a question about demand. The demand exists. It is not a question about vision. The vision has been written down, costed out, presented, and delivered. It is sitting in an inbox somewhere, or in a filing cabinet, or in the memory of a hundred people who attended a meeting where they were shown smoke instead of a plan.

It is a question about what we do now. This month. This year. While the roof still holds and the courts are still playable and the eighty-seven-year-old is still just a seventy-one-year-old who shows up on Tuesdays and Thursdays and reads the plaque on his way in.

Scrooge got a ghost. We don't. We get a choice, and we get it exactly once, and nobody is going to wake us up on Christmas morning and tell us it's not too late. It is not too late. But it will be. That is the thing about too late—it doesn't announce itself. It just arrives, quietly, the way a medical building arrives on a two-block stretch of Patterson Avenue, and suddenly there is a Subway where court three used to be and a kid on a bike who has never heard of you.

I have written these essays over the past year because the pen was the only instrument I had. I am not on the board. I don't run the Y. I don't control the money or the votes or the construction schedule. All I could do was write it down—the history, the numbers, the promises, the failures, the vision—and put it in front of anyone who would read it.

It is all on the record now.

The lady and the tiger are both behind their doors. Amber Lee is behind one of them, handing a membership badge to a young man who drove seventeen hundred miles because he heard this place was worth seeing. A three-story medical complex is behind the other, and an old man standing on the sidewalk trying to remember what it felt like to play on a Wednesday when everything still worked.

Appendices

Documents on the Record

————

Appendix A

Letter to YMCA Leadership — February 20, 2026
Hand-delivered five days before the February 25
community meeting.

Brian and Cindie,

I am writing as a thirty-year YMCA member and a former board member and board president regarding the February 25, 2026 meeting addressing the future of the Tennis Center.

The attached memorandum addresses matters of institutional commitment and stewardship. It outlines the historical foundations of the Tennis Center, the representations made to the tennis community in recent years, and the implications of the current course of action.

This is not a nostalgic objection to change. It is a governance issue. Community-built assets and explicit assurances carry consequences. How this matter is handled will affect more than a single program; it will shape the YMCA's standing as a trustworthy steward of donor-supported initiatives.

This matter will not self-resolve and should not be deferred. I look forward to a substantive discussion on February 25.

Sincerely,
Doug McCarty

————

The Eugene YMCA Tennis Center and Institutional Stewardship

This memo is neither about nostalgia nor resistance to change. It is about commitments—specifically, commitments that induced decades of funding, volunteer labor, loyalty, and trust, and that are now being set aside without consent or transparency.

In practical terms, the Eugene YMCA has departed from three foundational commitments to the Eugene tennis community. Two are historical. The third concerns the future. Together, they raise serious questions about institutional stewardship and the credibility of the YMCA as a partner in community-built assets.

The First Commitment — and the First Departure (Late 1970s)

The Eugene YMCA Tennis Center did not originate as a YMCA capital initiative. It was conceived, funded, and largely built by members of the local tennis community on YMCA land pursuant to a mutual operational understanding: the tennis community would raise the funds and build the facility; the community would continue to support it through membership, volunteer activities, and fundraising; and the YMCA would operate and maintain the facility as a tennis center for the benefit of the Eugene community.

For more than forty-five years, this understanding was honored in practice. The YMCA fulfilled its commitment, and the tennis community fulfilled its commitments. Tennis instruction, leagues, junior development, tournaments, and community programs flourished. Generations of Eugene residents passed through its doors. Our own family spans three generations on those courts.

The recent abandonment of the commitment to operate and maintain the facility as a true tennis center marks a unilateral departure from that foundational exchange of promises. The length of time the commitment was honored does not diminish its breach.

The Second Commitment — and the Second Departure (2022)

In 2022, during planning and fundraising for the new YMCA facility, members of the tennis community sought clarity regarding the future of the Tennis Center. Explicit assurances were given: the Tennis Center would remain; tennis programming would continue; and the historic relationship between the YMCA and the tennis community would be respected.

The tennis community relied on those assurances in good faith, and those assurances influenced continued financial, institutional, and emotional support for the broader YMCA project.

Subsequent actions diverged from those representations. That divergence constitutes a second departure—not from a decades-old understanding, but from recent and express assurances made during active strategic planning. That raises serious fiduciary questions.

The Third Commitment: The Future

From its inception, the Tennis Center represented an investment in the long-term recreational life of the city. Donors did not give for a short-term trend, or to build some sort of multi-purpose sports barn. Volunteers did not work for a temporary program. They invested in a durable vision—one in which future generations would have access to a dedicated tennis facility in perpetuity.

Repurposing the Tennis Center and effectively displacing the community that built and sustained it undermines not only past commitments but future trust. If the YMCA changes the fundamental terms of that long-standing arrangement unilaterally, the willingness of the community to support the Y currently, and fund or build future initiatives, will inevitably be affected. The damage to community confidence is already evident.

The building still stands. The question is whether the commitments that justified its existence still do.

Why This Matters Beyond Tennis

Charitable institutions do not endure on facilities alone. They endure on trust. For decades, the Eugene YMCA has benefited from a uniquely strong community relationship grounded in that trust.

When community members contribute money, labor, and loyalty to a project built on specific representations, the integrity of those representations becomes central to institutional credibility.

The YMCA's reputation in Eugene has long rested on the belief that it acts as a faithful steward of community-built assets. Decisions made in this matter will signal whether that belief remains justified.

———

Appendix B

The Eugene Y Tennis Academy — Proposal to YMCA Leadership

Delivered to Brian Steffen, CEO, March 11, 2026.

Dear Brian,

I'm writing to you about the future of the Y Tennis Center. I have given it quite a bit of thought and am attaching several documents that propose an exciting and innovative plan moving forward.

The way I see it, you are facing a difficult prospect—a Scylla or Charybdis choice which, it turns out, may be unnecessary after all. You preside over the continued degradation of the tennis center and get blamed for that, and the Y suffers for it. Or eventually the economic reality of the tennis center and its future downward trajectory ends with the sale of the entire parcel—worth perhaps $3 million today—to fund other projects in the area. And you still get blamed for it. But $3M spread across those projects will be almost a rounding error.

However, I see a relatively clear path forward which, with real vision and a little adventuring spirit, could accomplish four things simultaneously:

1. Position you as a visionary Y leader—not just in Eugene or Oregon, but nationally.

2. Create an innovative tennis academy that would find not only local support, but national sponsorship from brands like Nike, Wilson, Head, and the USTA—the kind of sponsorship a local Y simply cannot attract on its own, but that a nationally-positioned Tennis Academy anchored in a Big Ten athletic corridor could.

3. Get the management and operational headaches off your plate and onto the plates of the tennis community—people who have demonstrated 45 years of commitment to this facility and know how to run it.

4. Generate positive cash flow revenues to the Y for the next 30 years—funding programs and maintenance here and elsewhere in the Eugene/Springfield YMCA complex.

The Model Already Exists — One Mile Away

Before describing the Academy in detail, I want to draw your attention to something hiding in plain sight. One mile from the Tennis Center sits Hayward Field—arguably the most celebrated track and field venue in America. What the University of Oregon and the Eugene community built there did not happen by accident. It happened because a group of people had the vision to layer events: state high school championships, regional high school meets, college invitationals, NCAA Championships, and ultimately world-class professional and international competitions. Track Town USA is not a tagline. It is an identity built one event at a time, over decades, through exactly the kind of institutional partnership and community commitment we are proposing for tennis.

Financial Summary
1. Under current operations: estimated net loss of $100,000-$150,000 per year to the Y.
2. Under the Academy model (conservative): + $315,000 per year in facility fees—zero Y operational burden.
3. Under the Academy model (optimistic): +$585,000 per year—1,300 members, full program suite, regional and national tournaments.
4. 30-year Y revenue (facility fees only): $9.45M to $17.55M—depending on scenario.

What We Are Asking For
1. A genuine commitment to tennis as the sole and primary use of the tennis courts—beginning with full court restoration by Memorial Day.
2. The establishment of an Autonomous Governing Board (AGB)—with a YMCA representative as a full voting member, and a parallel commitment to seat a Tennis Center representative on the YMCA Board itself.
3. A formal commitment to begin work with the AGB on the Eugene Y Tennis Academy plan—with the understanding that the tennis community is prepared to help build, fund, and govern what it is proposing.

The full proposal, including the Vision and Concept Overview, Financial Model and Revenue Projections, and Three Paths Forward analysis, was delivered in its entirety to Brian Steffen on March 11, 2026.

———

Appendix C

Response from Brian Steffen, CEO — March 2026

The following is Brian Steffen's email response to the Academy proposal, reproduced in full, with author's annotations.

Doug,

Thank you for taking the time to share your overview, notes, opinions, and proposal.

I enjoyed reading through it and considering the vision you outlined.

[Author's note: The word "opinions" is doing quiet work in that first sentence. The proposal contained a detailed financial model, a governance structure, a construction plan, and a three-path comparative analysis. Categorizing it alongside "notes" and "opinions" reframes a formal business proposal as casual correspondence.]

I'm happy to share a bit of data with you, knowing that what I'll share is historical and does not impact your overall "conservative" or "optimistic" visions.

The Tennis & Pickleball programs at the Y do not have net losses; rather, they generate around $10,600 in positive net income per month; that is the monthly average since July 1, 2023. That number is inclusive of utility bills and supplies at the Center, but no percent of costs for admin or facility staff members are included. None of the Y's programs are fully "cost burdened" in our Statement of Activities. Meaning, we are not loading on portions of our overhead costs to programs.

[Author's note: Brian reports net income of $10,600 per month—$127,200 annually. He then discloses that no staff salaries are allocated to that figure. The Tennis Center is open approximately 5,000 hours per year with a minimum of two front-desk staff at all times, plus a director, two assistant directors, and a rotating roster of tennis coaches. At conservative estimates—$100,000 for director and assistants, $200,000 for hourly staff,

$30,000 for coaching and miscellaneous—the unallocated personnel cost is approximately $330,000. When you add the staff back in, the $127,000 surplus becomes approximately a $200,000 annual loss. This is worse than my original estimate of $100,000–$150,000, which Brian was attempting to refute.]

I don't know how you are arriving at your estimated cost of $2.32–$3.4 million for four new indoor courts, so I can't really speak to those values. I can say that I had four new indoor courts estimated by a local general contractor in September 2019 (a Butler-style building) and their estimate was $4.2 million (this was a 5-page line-by-line estimate . . . not an 'off-the-cuff forecast'). After the listening session I asked them to update their estimate because I'm curious what that value would be in 2026. At the same time this estimate was provided the new Y was estimated to cost $34 million (it ended up costing roughly $49M . . . a roughly 44% increase between September 2019 & May 2022 when the new Y's contracts were signed). If I applied that same cost escalator, the 2019 value would forecast out to a cost of $6,050,000 in 2022 . . . but I do not know how the local construction market has settled down since the new Y's contract was signed.

[Author's note: The new Y was estimated at $34 million and cost $49 million—a 44% overrun. Brian cites this as evidence that construction costs escalate. The reader may also note that it is evidence of the Y's own project management track record. Our proposal uses community-build methodology specifically to avoid the cost structures that produced a $15 million overrun on the Y's own facility.]

Importantly, their estimate was simply to create four new courts in a Butler-style building; it did not include other updates to the overall property. A few examples that have been on our mind and on Gro's mind:

— The existing stem walls of the current Center are leaking in several locations. We would like to have those leaks investigated and repaired. I have no idea what that might cost.

— We would like to add HVAC to the Tennis & Pickleball Center (and seal it up more overall) due to quite a bit of member feedback related to temps/allergies/smoke, and the potential to have it prepared as an emergency shelter in the event of an earthquake. We had local contractors estimate this last year and estimates ran from $250,000-$400,000.

— The existing courts were resurfaced during the 2016 remodel and need to be done again. Ideally courts would be resurfaced every 4-8 years. This usually runs $40k-$60k.

— The manufacturer of the lights in the Tennis & Pickleball Center is no longer in business and the lights are no longer made. Repairs are becoming costly and difficult. We would like new lighting.

— We would like to reside the Center and ensure it would match any future new development at that location.

[Author's note: This catalog of deferred maintenance —leaking walls, no HVAC, courts not resurfaced since 2016 (ten years overdue by the Y's own standard of every 4-8 years), obsolete lighting from a manufacturer no longer in business—is presented as a reason the Academy proposal may be insufficient. The reader may note that it is instead a detailed description of institutional neglect of the facility the Y was entrusted to maintain. Every item on this list occurred on the Y's watch.]

I am more than happy to share your vision and notes with the board. I know that our Board President met with a few tennis members today and they asked if a few of them could make a presentation at a future board meeting. He and I met this evening and he thinks he will introduce this question to the board during our next board meeting and see how the board feels about a potential presentation from a few folks at a future board meeting.

[Author's note: A proposal to see if the board will agree to consider whether to schedule a presentation at a future meeting. This is three layers of deferral in a single sentence.]

Today the Stathos Y is one of the busiest Ys in the country, serving over 18,500 members, and hosting over 900,000 visits per year. I believe the secret to its success is anchored in the idea that the community heavily influenced what the Y built and the programs it operates. The community informed the vision and we sought to fulfill that vision.

I believe the Y's future capital campaigns will be successful when they do all that they can to anchor back to the broadest community needs and to meet those needs through a lot of intentional work and planning.

[Author's note: "Broadest community needs" is the key phrase. It reframes the tennis community—which built, funded, and sustained the facility for forty-seven years—as a narrow special interest. The fifteen thousand future members who don't yet know they need this place are, by this logic, less important than the broader community's unspecified needs. This is the institutional language of displacement dressed in the vocabulary of inclusion.]